How To

MAKE MONEY GROWING PLANTS, TREES, AND FLOWERS

A Guide to Profitable Earth-Friendly Ventures

Dr. Francis X. Jozwik

ANDMAR PRESS
Mills, Wyoming 82644

Library of Congress Catalog Number 91-75621
ISBN 0-916781-22-4
Printed in the United States of America

CIP

Jozwik, Francis X.
    How to make money growing plants, trees, and
flowers; a guide to profitable earth friendly ventures /
Francis Xavier Jozwik.
    p.cm.
    Includes bibliographical references and index.
    ISBN 0-916781-22-4

    1. Horticulture 2. Small business–management.
    I. Title
SB50   635
                                    QB191-1388

CONTENTS

PART I
FUNDAMENTAL RELATIONSHIPS
OF HORTICULTURE AND BUSINESS

PART II
MONEY MAKING
BUSINESSES
IN HORTICULTURE

PART III
HOW TO GET STARTED
AND SUCCEED IN BUSINESS

4

ABOUT THE AUTHOR

Francis Jozwik received a Ph.D. in Plant Science from the University of Wyoming in 1966. He began his professional career lecturing in plant physiology with the University of Wisconsin System and later was appointed to the position of Arid Lands Research Scientist in the Commonwealth Scientific and Industrial Research Organization of Australia.

In addition to his scientific and academic background, Dr. Jozwik has become active in commercial horticulture as the owner of a successful greenhouse and nursery business. The wide experience Dr. Jozwik has acquired both as a scientist and in private industry assure that his books and articles are technically correct while possessing a down-to-earth style.

Who's Who In America has honored Dr. Jozwik for his professional accomplishments by repeatedly including his biography in that publication. The National Science Foundation has supported some of his basic research in the field of biosystematics.

Readers of the present book who wish to investigate specific details of commercial ornamental plant culture more thoroughly will find a larger volume entitled *The Greenhouse and Nursery Handbook* useful for further study. Ordering information for that title and others by Dr. Jozwik is available near the back cover.

DISCLAIMER

This book is intended to present information about commercial activity within certain subject areas of horticulture. While the author and publisher have carefully attempted to make this information reliable and timely, readers should note that a good deal of it is based upon personal experiences and observations of the author. The validity of the information and viewpoints can differ with circumstance; therefore, neither the author nor publisher guarantees the accuracy of the text material under all situations.

No attempt has been made to make the present book a final and ultimate source of information about the subject matter involved. Readers should always study further sources in order to complement, amplify, and confirm the present text.

Beginning a business in specialized horticulture is not a get rich quick scheme. Although many people have become extremely successful in this field, most have accomplished the feat only after working hard and smart.

The author and Andmar Press shall have no liability or responsibility to any individual or entity experiencing loss or damage, or alleged loss or damage, thought to be caused directly or indirectly by information presented in this book.

Readers who have purchased this book directly from Andmar Press and who do not wish to accept the above conditions in full may feel free to return the book to the publisher for a refund of the purchase price. The original Andmar Press invoice along with the customer's name and address must accompany all refund requests.

If you purchased the book from any independent agent other than Andmar Press, you must follow their refund procedures by contacting them directly for reimbursement.

Part 1

FUNDAMENTAL RELATIONSHIPS OF HORTICULTURE AND BUSINESS

AUTHOR'S NOTE

There are two primary reasons why a person should contemplate going into a particular field of business. First, the individual, by underlying nature, must hold a strong and abiding interest in the subject matter. Second, the field must offer a reasonable chance of monetary success. No sane person wants to spend their time doing something which holds no interest for them, and no one I know wants to run a business which doesn't make money.

Given the obvious nature of these two reasons for entering a business field, it is amazing how many people become involved in a venture which lacks one or the other, or both essential characteristics. I hope that after reading this book, you will be able to intelligently decide whether a horticultural specialty area can fulfill both necessary attributes when your particular situation is addressed.

How To Make Money Growing Plants, Trees, and Flowers is a result of more than 30 years of my experience as a commercial grower of ornamental plants. It is a practical guide which will help you get started successfully in some aspect of horticultural business.

How To Make Money Growing Plants, Trees, and Flowers is oriented towards people who wish to begin in this industry with as little monetary risk as possible. Therefore, most of the information presented will deal with situations applicable to small start up ventures rather than to larger, more complex enterprises. This book is meant to be used by ordinary people who want to grow plants for profit. Highly technical production and marketing methods are not emphasized since they generally have little relevance to the initial stages of a new business.

The information you need now to get started is quite different from what you may need later to address the more concrete problems of day to day business operation. Several specialized horticultural publications are listed in the Literature section at the back of this book.

In *How To Make Money Growing Plants, Trees, and Flowers*, I do not focus upon the specifics about how to grow plants for a profit. My objective at the moment is to provide the beginner with a concise and easily read overview which highlights important points quickly. In this way, readers will hopefully maintain a creative frame of mind unhindered by over attention to detail. I want to help you choose an area of horticultural business in which to specialize and then show you how to start a profitable operation as easily as possible.

I trust you will find the information presented in the following pages to be both interesting and profitable. Horticulture is a tremendously satisfying field which abounds with opportunity. Keep in mind that many million dollar horticulture ventures were born in the backyards of enterprising individuals just like you.

Not only my own business success, but also those of numerous associates who I have become acquainted with over the years are concrete proof of the "rags to riches" possible when a person truly enjoys their life's work.

Chapter 1

INTRODUCTION TO THE HORTICULTURAL INDUSTRY

Horticulture is not a particularly exact word. One person might place a topic within the confines of agriculture or perhaps botany, while another would argue that it properly belongs in horticulture. Most dictionaries describe horticulture as dealing with the activity of growing fruits, vegetables, flowers, or ornamentals. It is frequently referred to as both a science and an art. This definition agrees fairly well with the meaning of horticulture in this book, but with the important qualification that the areas of flowers and ornamentals will be emphasized more than those of fruits and vegetables.

This reduction in the scope of the topic mainly results from the fact that flowers and ornamentals are the highest value crops which are widely cultured. Consequently, they offer the business person a better chance of good monetary returns, even if only a limited number of plants are grown.

Certain topics dealing with fruit and vegetable production are included in this book, but they will be limited to those cases where production takes place under cover (greenhouse) or at least in very intensively-managed outdoor facilities.

The types of horticulture I want to concentrate on as potential business projects are those which require a good deal of specialized knowledge and control of crop conditions. Success in specialized horticultural crops depends to a large degree upon knowledge rather than upon generous amounts of luck, land, and money (which are the hallmarks of traditional field crops).

A person armed with little more than a few hundred dollars and the right knowledge can still start a profitable greenhouse or nursery. Contrast this with the hundreds of acres of high-priced land and expensive field machinery needed to run a modest farm. An investment of a million dollars or more is commonly required for a traditional farm operation which supports a modern family in reasonable comfort.

HORTICULTURE AN EXPANDING INDUSTRY

Ornamental horticulture (those aspects dealing with flowers, trees, groundcover, lawn and garden, interior decoratives, water gardens, and other such plants) in the United States is a booming industry, and, as with any dynamic situation, there are lots of opportunities for enterprising individuals. The demand for ornamental plants is generated mainly by trends in national lifestyle which will continue unabated. Everyone is becoming more ecologically-minded and more fully aware of the ethical and practical benefits which ornamental plants can add to

Tasteful landscaping consistently ranks as the least costly method of improving home values. This fact alone helps commercial horticulturists sell billions of dollars worth of goods every year.

human life and the environment. Reinforcing this change in basic national psychology, is the fact that, generally, both husband and wife work outside the home. The two-income family increases household income but reduces time available for outdoor and indoor gardening activities.

People want to enjoy plants and flowers more, but they have less time to do it. Professional horticulturists can now command an excellent income by providing time saving goods and services which consumers demand. Ornamental horticulture is no longer an infant industry which supplies the basics of seed, fertilizer, and perhaps a few bareroot shrubs and trees. A large volume and varied assortment of sophisticated horticultural supplies and

The garden products section of a major discount chain. Similar setups in supermarkets, discount stores, and other mass market outlets account for perhaps one half of horticultural sales. This particular display is neat and offers a reasonable selection of merchandise. These are rare qualities in this type of merchandising.

services have become more-or-less necessities of life to many people. Well over 1/3 of all lawns in the United States are mowed and fertilized by turf care professionals. Furthermore, only the most athletic and frugal homeowner is ever observed pruning their larger trees in modern times.

Virtually every ornamental tree and only a small proportion less of annual and perennial flowers are purchased from commercial growers rather than being started from cuttings or seed by the homeowner. Over $30 billion dollars worth of lawn and garden business is transacted each year in this country alone, and ornamental plants are the largest crops in several states (according to U.S. Department of Agriculture statistics).

ROOM FOR INDIVIDUALS
IN HORTICULTURE

Fortunately for the individual entrepreneur, relatively little of the horticultural production industry has been invaded by large corporations. Only in the area of hard goods (such as fertilizer and pots), have they made significant inroads. Anywhere there is money to be made, we can expect corporate management to investigate the possibilities, but the inherent variability of plants, their need for constant care, and the diversity of environments in which they are utilized is not the ideal situation for the standardized methods which mega business employs.

Large national corporations have tried to enter the plant growing segment of horticulture, but have, in general, pulled back out as they find that producing living organisms is more complicated than manufacturing stoves and refrigerators. By far, the greatest total number of greenhouses and nurseries throughout the United States are small to medium-size and are owned by individuals who sell a good deal of their product through their own retail outlet. Even the larger production facilities are most frequently owned by individuals or closely held companies.

Marketing of greenhouse and nursery crops was formerly accomplished almost entirely through the producer's own retail facility, or through numerous independent florists and garden stores. At present, a large part of ornamental plant products are sold by chain, discount, and food stores; hardware and department stores also do a significant amount of business.

For live plants and cut flowers as a whole, a little less than half are now sold through the nontraditional outlets (of course, this will vary greatly, depending upon the exact

A medium-sized retail bedding plant greenhouse and tree nursery. Individually owned operations like this account for about one half of retail horticultural sales. Most consumers consistently prefer to purchase garden products at these full service outlets, even though prices are generally higher than at self service locations.

nature of the product, geography, and demographic factors). Twenty or thirty years ago, independent operations were caught unprepared to market effectively against chain-type competition, but, at present, the independents seem to have adapted well, and many may even be benefiting from the wide and constant public exposure which flowers and plants receive at mass outlets.

Those independent retailers who have placed their emphasis on service, high quality, and new or unusual products seem to flourish now while the ones who tried to compete head-on in price terms with mass outlets have fallen by the wayside. And many growers of ornamentals have seized the opportunity to supply chain-type outlets. Of course, these growers must adapt to the mass market philosophy of high volume and generally lower price for the product. Often times in this situation, quality has suffered. Chains pressure the grower for lower and lower prices until factors essential for proper plant growth are sacrificed. Fortunately, most people in the industry have begun to realize the folly of this situation, and, in general, chain buyers are stressing quality more than in the past.

The marketing competition from chains and the mass production methods employed by their suppliers are certainly an area of concern for every independent grower. However, this situation has persisted for a long enough time to allow us to confidently predict that conscientious and innovative smaller growers will always have a market for good products.

We may summarize the general situation in ornamental horticulture by saying that it is an industry whose exceptional growth is due to fundamental and continuing changes in national psychology and living patterns. Individuals and small companies dominate the plant growing segment, while activity in the marketing phase is split fairly evenly between chain outlets and independent operators. Although plants and flowers are often distributed nationally, market prices are still determined primarily by local factors, and participants are more-or-less able to fix their own prices by providing different levels of quality, service, and selection. Ornamental plants, trees, and flowers offer an exceptional vehicle for good profits while the monetary requirements for starting in business are generally much lower than in the traditional commodity-oriented segments of agriculture and horticulture.

BASIC ORGANIZATIONAL PATTERNS IN HORTICULTURAL SPECIALTIES

If you carefully recollected the specific activity or the combination of activities of each horticultural business you have visited over the years and classified these memories into logical order, I believe you would arrive at basically the same industry organizational patterns which will soon be outlined. In the process you would, of course, find that there are many hybrid operations which do not fall neatly into any one area of activity. Although each particular horticultural area will be explored in more detail later, readers will benefit from having a concise preview of the industry right from the start.

Production

The production phase of horticultural specialty crops is a rather obvious aspect of the industry, although only a few readers may have had the chance to observe the actual workings of such a growing facility. Your closest experience with production operations most likely would be with a small neighborhood greenhouse or nursery, which was growing a portion of its merchandising needs while buying the rest from wholesale specialists. You are not likely to have visited the production locations of larger independent retailers or wholesale growers. Generally, the managers of these larger production operations must, out of necessity, limit the number of visitors so that work may continue without interruption.

Production facilities for horticultural specialty crops are as diverse as the particular needs of each crop and the ingenuity of the individuals growing it. There are different ways to solve cultural requirements, and the chosen solution may vary with materials available, climate, financing, individual inclination, and marketing objectives. The atmosphere at a production facility may range from one of complete dependence on technical methods, to the opposite attitude where success or failure depends upon vague "feelings" the grower may have about the needs of crops. Fortunately, most modern growers lean toward the first alternative as they become aware of the competitive advantages offered by efficient, reliable crop production methods.

The judicious use of economically justified technical production methods is essential in successful operations, but the time proven attributes of hard work, good decision making, and persistence are still the main ingredients necessary for growing plants profitably.

The size of production facilities in specialized horticultural crops ranges from tiny backyard setups to gigantic operations. Most fall into the small or medium-size range. There has been some tendency of late (particularly in the greenhouse field) for firms to expand quickly. This is only natural when growers see attractive markets without an adequate supply of products. But many growers have found that a larger business does not necessarily lead to greater profits and stability. Some growers are now beginning to question the wisdom of extremely rapid growth and are concentrating more on profitability rather than volume.

The primary driving forces for change in the production aspects of horticultural specialty crops are the decrease in the availability of cheap labor and the virtual explosion in the technological knowledge which is taking place. Any present day grower who does not take advantage of labor saving techniques and who does not keep abreast of new knowledge in the field, will soon find that it is impossible to compete with more progressive operations. It is absolutely essential for growers to keep themselves informed about all aspects of the industry, so that they may organize their production towards the most efficient use of resources.

As an example, production of spring garden transplants by smaller local greenhouses has been greatly simplified by advances in seedling, soil, and fertilizer technology. In older days, the local grower started seeds and cuttings in fall and early winter for plants that would be sold 6 to 8 months later. Needless to say, this method of operation required a good deal of labor and plant knowledge. Now, a grower may order all of the essential ingredients prepackaged to arrive a few short weeks before sale to the customer and needs only to arrange ready-to-bloom plants in their final containers.

In this way, a great deal more selling volume may be achieved with less production space and expertise. However, these prepackaged materials are expensive, and they are not the most cost effective method of operation in all situations. The local grower must evaluate all aspects of the equation to determine which new methods can profitably be employed under the specific conditions at hand.

Marketing

The important point to be made about marketing in horticultural specialty crops is that, luckily, it generally lacks a centralized character. Centralized marketing, whether it results from government, industry, or financial interests, always tends to limit the ability of individuals to determine and ask for the price they feel is proper for the merchandise. Centralized markets, such as auctions and government and industry sponsored marketing authorities, represent an easy means for growers to sell crops. But the passive acceptance of whatever price marketing organizations allow, does not usually lead to the highest possible profits for better growers. Centralized markets function best when a product possesses relatively uniform characteristics. If growers must tailor their produce to meet uniform standards, then there is little room left for individuals who wish to distinguish their product in the public eye. This is the primary reason why food and fiber farmers have generally realized low profit levels from their operations. Within the different classes of corn which have been established by market authorities, each farmer in a region receives basically the same price at any given time. There is little incentive for product differentiation under these conditions. In fact, there exists a bias against any variation.

A similar situation exists for most major commodity crops. So, while centralized marketing may function as a lubricant to effective national trading and distribution, it rarely benefits innovative growers who wish to offer products which differ from the standard version.

In my role as a grower of ornamental plants and flowers, I have often wished that I could be spared the

The basic bedding plant display at supermarkets reduces garden products to the status of common commodities. Quality and price are generally on the low end.

necessity of always finding a profitable market for my plants. This is the most difficult part of my job, and I would much rather spend time immersed in the delightful task of growing beautiful crops. However, when the yearly accounting of profits is done, I give thanks that conscientious and knowledgeable growers are able to ask for and receive prices which are much higher than the ordinary. Growing plants for a living is fun, but it soon becomes stale when the monetary rewards are slim or nonexistent. Creating profitable marketing channels through active participation in the selling process takes time, thought, and advance planning but is well worth the trouble.

A marketing plan is necessary for anyone who wishes to grow plants for a profit. You must sell what you raise in order to stay in business. The financial success of horticultural specialty growers is usually determined more by their ability to market crops effectively rather than by their prowess as growers. The proper order of business is to first devise a marketing strategy and plan for implementation, and then grow the crop. It must be emphasized that proceeding in the opposite manner is the

Similar plant varieties as in the preceding photograph with one major exception: plants are tastefully combined into planter arrangements which excite the customer's imagination. Independent operators can command top prices for beautiful material like this.

most common mistake of unsuccessful growers. It is possible to build a successful career in horticulture simply be selling what others produce; you need not grow a single plant. In fact, the marketing phase of horticultural specialty crops is normally a more financially rewarding endeavor than is growing the plants. There are several areas of horticultural businesses, such as flower shops and garden centers, where no crops are generally grown; the operation serves strictly or predominantly as a marketing entity. For people who possess the talent to market effectively, this type of operation often offers a means of entering the industry with less monetary resources than is necessary to begin actual crop production.

The essential points about where and by whom most horticultural specialty crops are sold has been previously mentioned. It is obvious that marketing of these crops is evolving a two-tier structure. At the bottom are mass outlets who deal primarily in products which are treated more-or-less as commodities: those which are sold in volume, those which exhibit some degree of uniformity within classes and can be easily handled and priced, and those which require a minimum of service. On the second tier are the independent outlets which deal in more than strictly the commonplace plants and products and which offer a maximum of service. This two-tier merchandising system is evolving because of natural forces in the market place. You should accept the reality of the situation and search for a place to fit in rather than trying to "buck" the system. As an independent grower, you will not be financially successful in head-to-head price competition with a nationwide chain. Mass outlets will likely fail if they try to offer a myriad of special products and services.

Chain store marketing of plants is not necessarily a bad thing for the horticultural industry. For example, it provides an avenue of sales for those growers who prefer to emphasize a more volume-oriented approach to ornamental sales. Furthermore, there are thousands of sales jobs created by chain store garden centers.

Growers focusing upon supplying chain stores must realize one important fact: the chains are almost always in the driver's seat in regards to the price paid for a product. This situation results because chains are bigger and more financially powerful than the growers who serve them. The wholesale price for mass market plants thus tends to be driven down unmercifully.

Services

Many of you will wonder why I am now preparing to discuss services as part of a book about growing plants and flowers for a profit. Stop and think carefully of various businesses which have some connection to horticulture, you will find that some of them offer very little in the way of tangible plant products; they sell a service, such as landscape design, plant care, or pest control. These are the more obvious aspects of service in the industry, but there is some degree of service offered with almost every plant sale. Even the least service-oriented mass outlets provide care tags with plants to help customers enjoy their purchase. At the other end of the spectrum, the price of plants or flowers at some upscale specialty shops is mainly dictated by the amount of special service connected with the purchase. Some outlets for horticultural products do not have a clear vision of the relationship which connects products and services. They do not know what they are selling. This type of confused situation can lead to disastrous consequences through not pricing merchandise to include the cost of services rendered, aiming products at the wrong economic class of purchasers, and many more merchandising mistakes. Smart marketers learn to evaluate service factors correctly and how best to use them to their advantage in particular business situations.

In the future, the marketing aspect of horticultural products by independent operators will increasingly be dominated by those who are devising creative ways to provide needed services along with the plant products they wish to sell. The days when a grower could simply offer marigold and petunia seedlings or bareroot nursery stock and expect customers to knock down the door are over. Customers desire and need added services to satisfy new lifestyles. They will go someplace else if you don't provide what they want.

An important advantage which service-oriented businesses enjoy is that the massive and well-financed chain stores are not particularly efficient at offering a variety of individual services. Thus, the price of these services does not become driven down so easily.

Integration of production, marketing, and service

At this point, you may be slightly confused by the description of the three different areas of activity within the industry. You are, perhaps, asking yourself why a book entitled *Make Money Growing Plants, Trees, and Flowers* should be emphasizing that the future lies in developing market skills and providing services, or that the real opportunities for individuals to make money lie not so much in growing horticultural specialty crops but in these related follow-up activities. This emphasis in no way downgrades the importance of the plant growing activities in the industry, but merely recognizes the fact that modern producers must also be reasonably proficient in the marketing and service sectors in order to become successful. Quality plants will always be the keystone of the industry, but they certainly do not comprise the entire picture.

An individual firm can prosper and expand while exclusively engaged in production, marketing, or horticultural services, but most operations successfully combine two or more aspects to a greater-or-lesser degree. The most stable, prosperous, and enjoyable operations to manage are those which are fairly completely integrated in a vertical manner. That is to say, the operation produces the plants, provides the necessary services, and markets the combination to the end consumer. This is the ideal situation in which the business controls all the factors which are in its sphere of influence. Of course, there are always such factors as climate, the national economy, and chance occurrences which no business can hope to influence. This book will be premised upon the assumption that whatever particular horticulture business venture you might engage in, it will be vertically integrated to the maximum degree possible under the prevailing circumstances.

Mother Nature (climate) continually modifies the conditions under which ornamental plants are grown, sold, and serviced. A business structure which is vertically integrated is better able to accommodate the constant changes in operational details which must be made due to weather conditions.

WHERE TO START IN HORTICULTURE

I have mentioned, in a general way, some horticultural areas which lend themselves to business activities. Perhaps now is the best time to point out specific enterprises which you may wish to consider and which will be discussed more fully in later chapters. Some of these possible ventures are more widely applicable, while others might be suitably adapted to only a few special situations. You are the only person who can decide which most closely fits your interests, capabilities, and business environment. The list of likely enterprises in Table 1 is by no means exhaustive and should be interpreted only as a starting point for inquiry. You will notice quickly that some of these business areas could be combined into a single operation if the proper circumstances were available.

There is no magic formula for deciding which horticultural specialty is best. Basically, you want to choose one which emphasizes the strong points of your personal situation while minimizing any weak points. Study the business activities in Table 1 so that as you read further, it will be easy to relate particular information presented to individual areas which you find interesting. Don't try to make any final selection at this point. As you become more familiar with the different subject matter, it is likely your mind will be unconsciously guided toward the best possible choice: at some point you will spontaneously realize what it is you want to concentrate your efforts upon. Most people who have read this book to the present point must have a serious interest in horticultural topics. Accordingly, these readers, either from practical experience or from reading and education, probably possess considerable knowledge about the subject. This is a definite advantage

Table 1

Some specific business activities in specialized horticulture. One or more activities may often be included in the same operation.

A. Greenhouse ornamentals for indoor and outdoor decoration.

B. Nursery ornamentals, mainly outdoor production.

C. Retail sales only, can include any aspect of specialized horticulture.

D. Perennial plant specialist, mainly herbaceous landscape plants.

E. Greenhouse vegetable, fresh fruit, and greens production for ordinary consumption.

F. Greenhouse herbs and unusual vegetables, either fresh or dried for use in specialized serving and cooking situations.

G. Market gardens, direct to consumer outdoor production of fruits and vegetables. Sometimes includes herb and flower production.

H. Herbs and medicinal plant production, outdoor culture for wholesale distributors.

I. Seed production for specialty crops, seed wholesaler and distributor.

J. Mail order specialist, mostly concentrated in sales of dormant herbaceous and woody landscape plants but may be any crop.

K. Outdoor and interior landscape, may include only design and consultation services but usually entails plant sales and installation.

L. Interior plant care, usually business and public installations.

M. Exterior plant care, ranges from simple lawn jobs to extensive technical services.

N. Lawn sod and plug production, may also include installation.

O. Wildflower seed and plant production, concentration upon those species perceived to represent less domesticated entities for a climatic area.

P. Christmas tree production and sales, may include associated Christmas items.

Q. Horticultural therapy and learning services. Clients may be at a disadvantage physically or mentally or may require only a normal learning or recreational program.

R. Commercial pest control for lawns, gardens, and trees.

S. Water garden installation and service.

T. Irrigation installations for lawns, gardens, and trees.

U. Photography of horticultural subjects for sale to magazines, advertisers, etc.

(cont.)

Table 1 (cont.)

V. Creation of horticultural information material. Can involve printed matter, videos, etc., for magazines, training courses, businesses.
W. Manufacturers of fertilizers, plant containers, decorations, and other accessories for garden use.
X. Plants and services for natural area restoration, includes ecological planning.
Y. Consulting and design services for individuals, businesses, and government entities.
Z. Laboratory testing of plants, soils, and other horticulturally related material.

if you want to go into business. Why not start in a field in which you have inherent interests and talents? Many of the basic requirements for success in commercial horticulture will seem like second nature if you have already amassed an extensive knowledge about the subject.

I have always been interested in plants, and, many years ago, I became a university professor and researcher in plant science. This occupation proved to be reasonably satisfying, but it always seemed that my life was somewhat sterile and lacked a strong feeling of contact with nature and my own subconscious needs. After a few years working as a scientist, I simply arrived at a rather immediate decision to quit and start my own greenhouse business. As time has passed, I now understand some of the forces that led me to that fortunate decision.

Many persons, like myself, are interested in plants primarily for the beauty and harmony expressed in the existence of organisms rather than the intellectual stimulation which results from a careful study of their chemical and physical properties. Horticulture has allowed me to live a life filled with both intellectual satisfaction and an artistic joy which proceeds from my work with beautiful, living creations.

Also, I find that the competitive stimulation of commercial life and the healthy physical work often required in horticulture serve as an elixir which purely intellectual activities cannot match.

The personal feelings I have just described may or may not be reasons which have some influence upon your decision to start a horticultural business. For those

The family business is a good place to start learning and earning. The author's daughter enjoys her work in the greenhouse and the money it provides.

individuals who feel some kind of kinship to such things, perhaps you will find it reassuring that feelings such as these can be a positive practical advantage for anyone entering horticultural business. It certainly doesn't hurt to have a spiritual life which is in tune with the practical activities of earning a living.

Now let us examine a few hardheaded business reasons which show why growing plants or flowers or other specialty crops might be a profitable venture for you. Gardening of various types is the most popular leisure activity in America. Couple this with the demand for horticultural produce which accumulates from floral use, the food industry, and other miscellaneous sources, and you can easily see that horticulture is a large and broadly-based field. Some commercial horticulture activity can be found in almost every neighborhood in the country. There is opportunity everywhere, not just in particular population centers.

Since the utilization of special horticultural crops is predominately tied to leisure time, special events, or luxury consumption, purchasers seldom have price uppermost in their mind as they shop. They are looking for that special plant, Christmas tree, or the most succulent tomato which will help to make their life more enjoyable. This situation provides high profits for those horticulturists who are able to efficiently and tastefully supply the special needs of their targeted market population. As was mentioned previously, the price of special horticultural products to end consumers may be many times that which is justifiable upon material costs alone. Specialized horticulture is characterized by high markups on merchandise. Think of it as brokering art. How much did the paint used in the creation of the Mona Lisa actually cost? A smart operator in this industry can make a considerable income without a huge or continuing investment. Many of the opportunities available in this field are unknown to the general public or the ordinary business community.

Of course, you can seldom expect to start a successful business without investing some money. I don't want to give the wrong impression by suggesting that you can profitably start growing and selling specialty crops with only the shirt on your back. Any venture chosen will require at least a minimum investment to get started, and, depending on how fancy you get, some will cost a lot. What needs to be emphasized here is that, due to various factors, it is much cheaper to get started commercially in specialized horticulture than virtually any other field. That is if you don't mind working hard and are willing to acquire the necessary specialized knowledge! I can't motivate you to work hard, but I can supply much of the information necessary for success.

Some aspects of horticulture are so ridiculously inexpensive in which to get a commercial toehold that there is no excuse for even lower income persons to say they can't afford to get started. Under the right circumstances, you can literally turn a few cents of seeds into hundreds of dollars worth of plants which people are anxious to buy. All it takes is time and effort. More detail about some of these possible ventures will be given later.

The "rags to riches" possibilities just mentioned are based upon practical experience in my own business and the hundreds of success stories I have observed personally over the years. Any person who is highly motivated and has a sincere interest can succeed in a commercial horticultural business.

Another factor which might bear upon your entry and continued success in specialized horticulture is that, except in certain circumstances, there isn't a whole lot of foreign competition to deal with. Horticultural produce is often heavy and cannot normally be shipped profitably from country to country. Besides, disease and insect quarantine laws are tightly enforced and greatly restrict the free flow of imports. Sometimes, because of transport problems, you may face little competition even from operations only a few miles away.

I could write many more pages about general advantages characteristic of specialized horticulture, but I think you will benefit more by moving along so that we may soon investigate several concrete examples of interesting specific enterprises. Hopefully, I can help develop your knowledge to the point where you can make an informed decision about venturing into this thriving and exciting industry.

Personal Note from the Author:

A good deal of my success in the horticultural industry results from viewing the competition realistically and then devising means of building a strong business which minimizes direct competition with either mass marketers or other independent operators.

The least successful people in this industry are those who constantly blame their failure upon "too much competition" or "low price, low quality competitors". These constant complaints distract the business person from aggressively developing methods of dealing with normal competitive influences which always have and always will be a part of the free market system. This capitalistic system is why the United States continues to possess the most vibrant economy in the world.

Chapter 2

THE BUSINESS OF BUSINESS IS BUSINESS

Certain basic factors should be considered by anyone who is thinking about starting a business, no matter what the nature of the product or services which may be involved. Only those who have started and operated their own independent business can truly appreciate the massive effect this experience has upon the life of the person involved. Therefore, each individual must take such an important step carefully and with eyes wide open.

WHAT IS A BUSINESS?

The first point we must be perfectly clear about is this: exactly what definition is to be given to the word "business"? In the sense which we are using this book, I take business to mean "a series of actions or processes in which people engage to realize monetary profit." There are various qualifying remarks which we may wish to place upon this definition, such as: at what times during the life span of a business must it be profitable to qualify as a true business venture? The Internal Revenue Service is acutely interested in this point. I believe the IRS expects a business to be profitable one out of every four years to be eligible for tax treatment in this category unless extenuating circumstances can be proven to apply. Particularly in the start up phases of a business or in prolonged general economic downturns, it is not uncommon to find companies which operate at a deficit for several years running. By whatever details of definition which we restrict or expand upon the word, most of you will accept, in broad terms, the meaning which has been placed before you.

So we may see that whatever similarities a business possesses with other activities in our life, it is always characterized by the attempt to make a monetary profit. Many people who say they are in business are really engaging in a hobby or recreation. Their chief objective in these cases is to occupy their time with interesting or stimulating activities, not to earn a profit. In some cases, we find that individuals successfully combine business, hobby, and recreation. Certainly this is the most desirable circumstance. Some will argue that amassing money is not the sole object of business. I agree. However, we must have a primary objective by which to measure our definition or the attempt becomes meaningless.

We are spending so much effort to clear up our understanding of business because it is crucial for anyone who becomes involved in such an activity to understand exactly what it is they wish to accomplish. If you want to alter the definition which I have offered, by all means do so, but be aware of the change in goals and objectives which this change necessarily imposes. I have observed many unhappy people who, although thinking they are in business, are actually engaging in recreational and hobby activities which almost certainly preclude any chance of profit. Yet they continue to measure their success or failure by the profit yardstick. If they would look at their activities differently (that is to say with no connection to profit), they might find that their activities (and their life) were indeed enjoyable and satisfactory. If business, hobbies, and recreation are to be combined satisfactorily into a single activity, each component must be given its due importance and consideration in the overall objectives of the undertaking.

So, before you think seriously about getting into business, do some soul searching. Decide exactly what it is that will make your life more enjoyable, and how you think this may best be accomplished. Define goals carefully, and see if they make sense when considering the circumstances under which you live. In short, give careful consideration to the old adage "know thyself."

Not only must you evaluate how a business venture will affect your own individual life, but the impact upon the lives of others who are closely associated with you must be considered. Here we are speaking primarily of family members or those who have a legal connection of some sort to you. The long hours and material sacrifices often required to get a venture off the ground can be extremely taxing to personal relationships. Furthermore, the money aspects of a business must be viewed with an eye toward the legal implications involved. Most people have some small appreciation of how difficult it is to begin a successful business, but not many recognize that getting out of a business can be agonizing both monetarily and psychologically; this is particularly true if the venture has proven unsuccessful after a lengthy and costly attempt. This is just one more reason to thoroughly think through any decision about going into business. I am not trying to discourage you. In fact, I am attempting to offer the encouragement and information needed, but it would be less than honest to neglect pointing out some of the more sobering aspects of venturing into a commercial pursuit.

LEARN DETAILS OF PLANNED BUSINESS FIELD

Now, let's assume that you've carefully evaluated the general comments just presented and still think you are interested in starting a horticultural business. However, being the cautious type, you want to gather more information in order to make the most prudent and final decision possible. Where and how can the information you need be found? Some of the more useful and easier sources to utilize will be pointed out in the following discussion.

My all time favorite suggestion for learning about a field of business is: learn and earn at the same time. Go to work in the chosen industry in any capacity for which there is an opening, even if it means being the least respected and lowest paid member of the organization. You can have your laughs later when you start a successful competing operation. Right now the main objective is to learn as much as possible by the fastest and least expensive method available. Working for someone else will normally be the best way of accomplishing this objective. And while you are working, try to gain as wide a background as possible

— volunteer for all types of duties, no matter how distasteful. Each new experience will save time and money in the future. There is simply no better training available for the new business person than actually working in the field. And you get paid for it!

Of course, you can't learn everything necessary by working for someone else. Who knows, they might be doing a lot of things incorrectly. If you didn't find this out by picking up additional information from other sources, you might go on for years repeating the errors of your previous employer.

Another valuable fact finding tool is to visit all of the existing businesses you can that fall into the same general field. A lot of new ideas will be picked up in this way. The best method of making a fact-finding mission is to do a lot of looking around and listening, then make up your mind about the implications of these observations. Don't advertise that you plan to be in competition, and don't rely much on other people's opinions – as they may be mistaken or just making idle talk to pass the time.

Speaking to people in other fields of business is more likely to yield straight answers. They won't view you as a competitor. Remember, you need knowledge not only about your own specialty, but on how to do business in general. Local businesses will be able to give advice about the immediate climate for your new venture. Of course, it is imperative to interpret what you hear from these people with caution.

Several private and government agencies probably offer free or low cost business advice and counseling in your town. The Small Business Administration, farm loan boards, economic development boards, the Chamber of

Commerce, banks, and higher education facilities are but a few of the more obvious sources for help. It may well be that these people are perhaps not so enthusiastic about your project as you are since they are not personally involved and because, by their very nature, organizations such as these tend to become cautious. They will emphasize formal business plans and ask for quantitative data about production, marketing, and financing. Don't become irritated by the questions they ask: if your planned venture can't stand careful scrutiny by the bankers and bureaucrats, perhaps it is prudent to give it a second look.

The Internet offers access to a wealth of information both about general business and horticulture. Contact the web sites of obvious sources such as The Small Business Administration, universities, the Chamber of Commerce, and horticultural organizations.

There are private business consultants for hire, but they are expensive. Furthermore, the advice they are prepared to give will likely apply to larger and more formally structured operations than the one you will begin initially. Besides, you can usually buy a book for under fifty dollars that will give you similar information in more detail.

I am a firm believer in the value of higher education. However, let's face it: the true value of advanced education lies not in preparing an individual for a particular job, but in molding a society of individuals who have acquired the ability to think logically and critically in a variety of circumstances. So, my advice is that if you wish to lead a more fulfilling life in general, or if you have plans to advance further than a small private business, formal education may certainly be helpful. Yet, this is seldom a cost-effective method for small private business people to learn the details about a new venture they plan to start. Notice I wrote "cost-effective." You can probably learn what you need to know through formal education, but couldn't it be done more quickly and economically by other methods? Certain avenues to higher education are quite inexpensive. Night school or community college courses which fit into your normal working schedule are examples. On the other hand, a degree program at an out of town college or university can easily cost $35,000 per year in lost wages, room and board, and fees.

Every industry has trade shows, conferences, seminars, and professional publications. The world of specialized horticulture is certainly awash in them. And they are invaluable to the newcomer. Publications are by far the most cost-effective way to learn about the industry. For less than the cost of a daily newspaper, you can subscribe to three or four industry magazines and keep abreast of all of the new plant varieties, products, prices, and research developments in your particular field. Most of the books needed will be available in a nearby public library, and the ones that aren't may be purchased at a relatively low cost. The literature section at the back of this book contains some publications which should be considered for your private library.

Trade shows and seminars are expensive, especially if held out of town, but tremendously enlightening. If you have time to wait, keep an eye on the industry calendar in trade magazines, and very likely you will find shows or other gatherings which will periodically take place in the nearest large city. Trade shows enable you to evaluate a lot of products and services and make business contacts quickly. The value of educational seminars and conferences

ALLIED NURSERY TRADE SHOW
July 17-20, 2000
Phoenix Civic Plaza
Phoenix, Arizona, USA

It will all be here – hot new plant materials, the latest products and equipment, and innovative services and technologies. This year's show will be larger than ever – plan to stay awhile!

Advertisements for major professional horticultural organizations often appear in trade publications. You can learn a lot in a hurry by attending meetings such as this.

varies widely, depending upon the quality and nature of the presentations.

Most people starting a business are too poorly informed or too lazy to thoroughly research all the information they need **before** beginning an operation. If you follow the simple recommendations set forth in this book, you could save thousands of dollars and untold hours by approaching the proposed venture in a businesslike manner rather than relying on vague hunches and hopes.

EVALUATE INFORMATION GATHERED

After making a reasonable effort to educate yourself about business in general and about your particular field of interest, examine all of the information realistically. Try to avoid looking at your plan through rose-colored glasses. Quantify information whenever possible, numbers are less likely to lead you astray than are vague impressions and general statements. Write down all your important conclusions. You will want to refer to this information later. Now comes the moment of truth! Does all the preparation and investigation still indicate your business will fly? If not, you had better weigh all the risks and benefits more carefully before jumping in with both feet. See if there may be some way to test the venture without an all-out commitment of time and resources.

If applicable, see if the business can be started in several steps — with the next step following only after the previous one has proven successful. This approach limits your risks considerably. It also helps to develop a written list of business options to aid in choosing between competing ideas and different methods of reaching your ultimate goals.

The final decision is yours alone to make. You cannot gather enough information to assure a completely error-free choice. The final step will always remain a reflection of personal desires and beliefs. Don't force a decision; if the question is turned around in your head enough, the answer will usually come without a conscious effort. You will simply know what it is you must do.

Let me say something before we pass on to the next topic. Some of the greatest inventions, revolutions in thought, and material achievements of man would not have been accomplished by the people responsible if they had paid much attention to negative information which indicated their projects were hopeless. If you still feel competent to begin a business in horticulture after serious investigation shows it has little likelihood of success, go ahead and do it anyway, but make the plunge with a clear understanding of the odds you face.

Personal Note from the Author:

Doing the necessary background work and number crunching before starting a new project may sometimes be tiresome. The natural human tendency is to just jump in and hope everything works out. This way of operating is less work to begin with but often leads to unpleasant failures.

After many years of self-observation, I have found that the failures experienced in any venture greatly (in psychological terms) outweigh any small benefits in time saving that may have been realized in shoddy planning.

In other words, I am the type of person who cannot forgive myself for major losses. Are you? If not, then be sure to do your homework before making major business decisions.

Chapter 3

THE FIRST STEPS OF A NEW BUSINESS

Now that you have decided to go into business, and believe that horticultural specialties may well be the most opportune field, what is the next step towards making this dream a reality? I believe you must focus attention upon a definite niche within this diverse industry. No business could operate successfully in all the various activities of specialized horticulture. You must specialize even further in order to concentrate available time and resources upon a manageable undertaking.

CHOOSING A FIELD OF SPECIALIZATION

Three important questions must be answered in the process of choosing a definite business activity area. First, what field of activity interests you the most? *This is the key question.* No one can put forth the tremendous effort necessary to start a business for long if they are not fervently interested in the field. If you can't decide between two or three possibilities, perhaps this means you should combine them into a single larger enterprise — a quite common solution. Second, which of the choices looks like it will make the most money with the least effort? Let's face it, we are talking about a business, not a recreational or charity activity. Monetary success will be one of the primary measures of how good you are as a business person. Third, what is possible under the circumstances in which you live? Although a certain field of activity may be extremely interesting and appear as though it will make the most money, it may be nearly impossible to consider because it clashes with unchangeable aspects of your present life. You may have to settle for second choice under these circumstances. Life doesn't work out in the best possible way all the time; one must make compromises.

As you ponder these questions, keep in mind that your evaluation may change somewhat as more experience is gained. Try to avoid boxing yourself into situations that cannot be altered later if conditions or available information change.

THE QUESTION OF PARTNERS

People are social animals. They live together, eat together, fight together, and love together. Isn't it natural that they should be in business together? Perhaps so, but there are some important things you should consider before taking on a business partner. In some aspects, a business partner has more call upon your time, financial assets, and future happiness than does a partner in marriage. It is often almost impossible to disassociate oneself from an unsuitable business partner without major financial and legal difficulties.

So why would anyone want a partner? Well, some people just don't like to do anything by themselves. This is probably a good enough reason to take on a business partner if you feel really strongly about it. Personally, I think the wisest course is to avoid business partners unless they definitely add specific mental or material assets which are critical to the success of the venture. The decision to become partners with someone must be evaluated with an eye to the future. People seldom stay the same over long periods of time, and your agreeable partner of today may become the Frankenstein of later years. Almost everyone suffers some major personal problems over a lifetime which will significantly affect close associates or family. Can you deal with that? Although business partners can be a joy, like a good spouse they must be chosen carefully for the long haul.

You also need to understand that a close partnership can also affect your relationship with a spouse or immediate family. Sometimes a family feels "left out" as you develop ties with another individual.

INVENTORY OF RESOURCES AND LIABILITIES

Good business persons must be constantly aware of the material, monetary, and mental assets of the operation they manage. And they must keep track of the liabilities, both actual and potential, to which the business is subject. A good part of a manger's job is to make sure the sum total of the assets always exceeds the actual and potential liabilities. This is a difficult balancing act because it is not always possible to match like with like on both sides of the equation. You must often assign a common value measure

Table 2

Resource or liability category (actual and potential)	Value assigned	
	+	**−**
Personal financial condition. Personal health. Personal knowledge of field. Personal skills related to field. Personal work and organizational habits. Personal business experience. General educational level attained. Positive relationships in community. Spouse in agreement with objectives. Immediate relatives may help. Community business climate. Present business competition. Possible demand for product. Possible loans or grants available. Good labor pool available. Suitable business locations available.		
Total ±values in categories		
Grand total when ±values are combined.		

Higher positive grand total value indicates business is more likely to succeed. Negative grand total indicates you should evaluate going into business more carefully.

Suggested model for inventory of resource and liability categoroies affecting business start up: Assign each category an estimated value on a numerical scale of ±1 to 5. Give the largest + or − value to those categories in which you are more informed concerning the reliability of information. For example: If you are in excellent health, assign +5; if your health is very poor, assign −5.

to different assets and liabilities so they may be related logically to one another.

An accurate inventory of assets and liabilities is especially important for someone just staring out in business. It is necessary to know what you have to work with before making any critical decisions. The best way of actually visualizing your situation is to write down all existing assets and liabilities in separate columns. Then assign numerical values to each liability or asset. Total the numbers in each column to see if your assets outweigh liabilities. This exercise accomplishes several purposes: It makes you think carefully about just what your assets and liabilities are; it makes you compare their relative values; and it lets you know what the overall situation is. Do the same thing for assets and liabilities not yet in existence but which are likely to be a reality in the near future. Potential assets and liabilities can be used in your assessments of total net values, but they certainly shouldn't be given equal weight with present actualities. One possible means of evaluating the relationship of resources and liabilities is shown in the previous graphic example (Table 2).

Don't forget, we are not just talking about concrete assets and liabilities. If you have a good deal of knowledge about the anticipated field of business, this should be counted as one of your most valuable assets. And vice-versa — no experience is a negative point. When evaluating your existing financial condition there are standard forms which can be obtained to organize the information (an example from the Small Business Administration is pictured in the following pages).

MANAGE WITH A PLAN

Many tasks, when looked at for the first time, appear to be so complex or so large as to be overwhelming. This is a normal reaction, but it doesn't have to prevent you from accomplishing important objectives in life. Each problem you face is actually a collection of smaller, simpler problems. The way to solve an unmanageable problem is to break it down into manageable segments and work each one out individually. Starting a new business is a tremendous undertaking. The complexity of it will often lead to a paralyzing sense of inadequacy unless you break the task down into several parts and then develop a written plan of action and a written timetable for accomplishing each portion of the business start up. Once the plan is down on paper and the first mini-problem is resolved, you will feel the anxiety and inadequacy begin to melt away. This method is so effective that you will want to keep it in mind for later use when other large projects are started in your business enterprise. Each problem solving plan must be adapted to the specific developmental phases of the project at hand; in other words, there may be plans within the plan. Right now, you should be concerned with an overall strategy for handling the various projects necessary to get your new business off the ground. Begin by devising a master plan into which all of the sub-plans will fit as they are developed.

A master plan is not normally concerned with details. It should provide broad principles of organization, directions and means of action, and an appropriate timeframe for implementation. Specific undertakings, such as building a facility for your new business to function in, may then be worked out in detail and inserted into the master plan.

Think the business plan out carefully, and then stick to it as religiously as possible. There is no sense in developing an outline for your business progress if it is whimsically altered for the slightest reason. Of course, even the best plans may require some changes to meet unforeseen circumstances, but changes should originate from a previously conceived method of integrating new data into the original plan. For some reason, people who like to grow plants don't seem adept or inclined toward formally planning their business goals and strategies. This is a big mistake! I have seen many plant businesses fail because of poor planning.

What are your goals?

- Exactly what kind of business do you want to create? Retail? Wholesale? Combination? Service Business?, etc.
- Are certain values more important than profit in your business philosophy?
- How do you want the community to envision you and your company?
- Can you write a clear statement of business goals in 25 words or less?

Factors influencing your business

- List the three main positive strengths your firm will possess.
- List the three main weaknesses which may hinder your firm's progress.
- What will make your business special in terms of competitive advantages?
- Where can you get reliable information upon which to base business decisions?
- What financial resources do you have now? Are there future possibilities of access to capital?
- What other concrete resources do you possess (land, education, health, buildings, vehicles, etc.)?
- List the specific group or groups of customers you expect to have as a clientele.

- How is the general business climate in your location? Is there serious competition for your chosen customer base?
- Who will staff the new business? Are the people available for primary positions capable and well-versed for their responsibilities?
- Is your family behind you?
- Are there any serious risk factors which may endanger your venture?

Strategy

- Is there a plan to capitalize upon the strengths and de-emphasize the weaknesses of your firm?
- What is the time frame allowed for accomplishing your overall goals?
- List the three fundamental aspects of business which must guide every decision you make (examples might be: customer service, product quality, profit, risk).
- Define how much capital and work you are willing to put forth. Have you set limits on the amount of risk to be tolerated?
- What percentage of monetary return is acceptable as a reward for your investment in work and capital? Be sure to arrive at a numeric value.
- Do you have a formalized long range marketing plan? Does it include specific numerical projections?
- Do you have a formalized long range production plan? Does it include specific numerical projections?
- What is your overall plan for fulfilling labor needs?
- Do your personal expectations and aspirations coincide with business goals?

Getting things done

- How is each particular goal or strategic objective to be reached? Write a short synopsis for future reference.
- When will each specific goal be accomplished?
- Who will be responsible for specific goals?
- How much will each objective cost? Set up a budget for every major business category.
- How will you know when each objective is achieved?

Assessment of progress

- Have you reached each objective?
- If not, what is the status?
- Is the direction properly set?
- Should the course of action be changed?
- Should you continue with this project?
- Have conditions changed enough to warrant updating the business plan or completely revising it?

SUCCESS TAKES TIME

Many people start a business with the unrealistic hope of becoming rich overnight. I want to caution that, even in a booming industry like ornamental horticulture, it will generally take 2-5 years before the business becomes truly profitable. You may find that the seed money used to start up and a reasonable owner's wage can be paid out earlier, but don't count on any extra profits for a few years. This is one of the main reasons why start up businesses fail—they did not budget properly for the extended time it usually takes to get off the ground.

I'm not saying success can't come very quickly if you hit some lucky circumstances, but it is safer to expect a few bumps in the road before reaching your final destination. Most business persons find that they become successful by adding small profit centers over the years. It takes time to discover and implement money making programs—but the end result is well worth the effort.

One good way to assure financial success and make it happen sooner is to develop habits of thought and action which inevitably lead toward that goal. A few individuals are naturally talented in this respect, but most people (including myself) must learn these habits through hard experience or through the counsel of others.

PERSONAL FINANCIAL STATEMENT

U.S. SMALL BUSINESS ADMINISTRATION

As of _____ , 19 ____

Complete this form for: (1) each proprietor, or (2) each limited partner who owns 20% or more interest and each general partner, or (3) each stockholder owning 20% or more of voting stock, or (4) any person or entity providing a guaranty on the loan.

Name   Business Phone

Residence Address   Residence Phone

City, State, & Zip Code

Business Name of Applicant/Borrower

ASSETS	(Omit Cents)	LIABILITIES	(Omit Cents)
Cash on hands & in Banks	$	Accounts Payable	$
Savings Accounts	$	Notes Payable to Banks and Others	$
IRA or Other Retirement Account	$	(Describe in Section 2)	
Accounts & Notes Receivable	$	Installment Account (Auto)	$
Life Insurance-Cash Surrender Value Only	$	Mo. Payments $	
(Complete Section 8)		Installment Account (Other)	$
Stocks and Bonds	$	Mo. Payments $	
(Describe in Section 3)		Loan on Life Insurance	$
Real Estate	$	Mortgages on Real Estate	$
(Describe in Section 4)		(Describe in Section 4)	
Automobile-Present Value	$	Unpaid Taxes	$
Other Personal Property	$	(Describe in Section 6)	
(Describe in Section 5)		Other Liabilities	$
Other Assets	$	(Describe in Section 7)	
(Describe in Section 5)		Total Liabilities	$
		Net Worth	$
Total	$	Total	$

Section 1. Source of Income		Contingent Liabilities	
Salary	$	As Endorser or Co-Maker	$
Net Investment Income	$	Legal Claims & Judgments	$
Real Estate Income	$	Provision for Federal Income Tax	$
Other Income (Describe below)*	$	Other Special Debt	$

Description of Other Income in Section 1.

*Alimony or child support payments need not be disclosed in "Other Income" unless it is desired to have such payments counted toward total income.

(Use attachments if necessary. Each attachment must be identified as a part of this statement and signed.)

Name and Address of Noteholder(s)	Original Balance	Current Balance	Payment Amount	Frequency (monthly, etc.)	How Secured or Endorsed Type of Collateral

SBA Form 413 (2-94) Use 5-91 Edition until stock is exhausted. Ref: SOP 50-10 and 50-30   (tumble)

This form was electronically produced by Elite Federal Forms, Inc.

An example of data which can help in making business decisions. This is the first page of a two page financial statement. Similar forms can be obtained from any bank or the Small Business Administration website.

QUANTIFY PLANNING WHENEVER POSSIBLE

At some point it will be necessary to begin planning the individual aspects of your horticultural business in greater detail. Depending upon the subject, some plans will be more adaptable to numerical representation and analysis than are others. If you are planning a greenhouse facility, it is quite easy to arrive at a fairly exact cost estimate since the prices of various components are readily available. Such things as the relative merits of different plant varieties are more difficult to express in a numerical format because they are generally described with only words or phrases. It is possible, however, to assign numerical values to various plant characteristics and thereby rank different varieties in a quantitative fashion. You could then devise a crop plan which allows a choice between different varieties by comparison of numerical values assigned to them.

You must be the judge as to when a quantitative analysis of various problems is possible or justifiable. Some situations are simply not easily expressed in numerical terms with any degree of precision. I am not of the opinion that it is useful to quantify every aspect of the decision making process, but I am suggesting that a strong reliance upon numerical expression in appropriate circumstances will lead you to more satisfactory solutions. Numbers are more precise than words and, hence, less subject to multiple interpretations. There is some truth in the old business adage which says "the numbers don't lie."

Sure, it is hard work to slog through a financial statement, tediously certifying and inserting, in monetary terms, each detail of your material life. However, the end result is more precise than simply saying "I feel rich" or "I feel poor." The bottom line of a financial statement represents only one of many benefits. With all material assets neatly expressed in numerical terms, the strengths and weaknesses in your financial life can be more easily evaluated. Decisions can then be initiated which will correct any imbalances.

Monetary information is not the only data which is expressed in an exact numerical format. If you are growing crops in the greenhouse or field, draw up a complete projected mathematical outline of what space crops will occupy throughout their growth, the quantity of different materials they will need for production, how many you plan to sell at different times, and so on. All of this numerical data can be used as an aid in crop scheduling and to produce a rather accurate estimate of crop profitability. An example of this process will be presented in a later chapter dealing with greenhouse crops.

Quantitative data is useful for your own planning, and it is an absolute necessity when dealing with financial institutions and agencies. They simply will not talk to you about loans or grants without seeing a well thought out financial and business plan. Generally, the more numbers you give them, the happier they are.

EVALUATE BUSINESS PROPOSITIONS CAREFULLY

In the process of choosing a field of horticulture in which to do business, you will likely encounter several ready-made propositions which offer a sure-fire business venture without much work or knowledge on your part. The only way to separate the wheat from the chaff is to investigate any proposition carefully and logically. Don't believe any unsubstantiated claims which, upon reflection, do not make sense.

Certainly you do not want to discount all business propositions just because they did not originate as your own idea or because they propose to offer you knowledge and services for a fee. Some of the greatest business successes of postwar decades have been built upon such a concept; this is the franchise plan. Before you turn loose of any hard-earned cash, make sure the proposition is reputable by checking out the background of the offering parties and by demanding references from existing customers.

I have only one further comment about prepackaged business propositions: The offering parties might be reputable and have previous customers who are happy and prosperous, but the deal simply may not be applicable to your circumstances. Standardized success formulas do not work in every case. Only you can be the judge.

Personal Note from the Author :

  The importance of writing down and believing in a business plan is illustrated by my own plant business start up. I created a rather detailed advance financial picture for the first few years of operation. It was based upon selling plants primarily to florists and supermarkets at wholesale. The hypothetical financial plan showed that enough profit to survive could not be made by selling strictly wholesale — there weren't enough potential wholesale customers in the locale to generate an adequate volume of sales.

  I chose not to believe these figures because I wanted to start a growing operation — not a retail/ growing combination. So, the figures were disregarded, and a wholesale operation was started anyway (damn the torpedoes, full speed ahead).

  Needless to say, the numbers were right, and after 2 years in business I was forced to begin a retail emphasis in order to stay solvent. If the business plan had been followed from the outset, it would have saved me 2 years of hard, unprofitable work.

Part II

MONEY MAKING
BUSINESSES
IN HORTICULTURE

This section will outline some money making horticultural businesses which might strike your interest. The main objective is to let you know the variety of opportunities available, not to provide detailed operational plans for any particular enterprise. Although I have been exposed to numerous aspects of the horticultural industry over the years, there are some limitations to my presentations because no one could be an expert in all aspects of any particular horticultural field, much less in all the fields to be touched upon.

Another reason I have limited my discussion of various fields is that I feel they offer potential in only a limited range of circumstances. Obviously, greenhouse and nursery production and horticultural retailing are well-developed in most parts of the country because there is a broad demand for these products and services. It makes sense to devote most of our attention to these topics because there is opportunity in almost every neighborhood. Success in some more specialized horticultural businesses may only be possible under specific circumstances of geography, climate, population, or other conditions.

Any presentation where numerous fields are considered must, of course, be greatly generalized. If you become especially interested in any specific horticultural area, please realize the need to acquire a good deal more information about it than is presented in the following pages.

As you examine potential business areas, be sure to focus upon those which interest you greatly, not only upon those which seem as though they would be good money makers. Almost all of the extremely successful people I know in this industry are following a personal dream — their business makes money mainly because the owner is naturally interested in and enthusiastic about the chosen field.

Chapter 4

PRODUCTION AND MARKETING OF GREENHOUSE ORNAMENTALS

Production of ornamentals under some type of protective structure is nothing new. Even ancient cultures engaged in this practice as early as suitable building materials and engineering expertise became available. There are numerous archeological indications that ancient Egyptian, Greek, and Roman cultures grew plants in structures akin to our greenhouses. Until fairly recent times, however, most greenhouses were constructed for private use of well to do individuals such as European royalty. Perhaps only in the past 200 years has there developed a serious commercial aspect to this age-old preoccupation. Most growth in the industry has taken place since the beginning of the 20th century. The pace of construction, production, and demand seems to currently be expanding at an ever increasing rate.

It is hard to know whether this fevered pace is fueled by new production and construction technology which allows greenhouse growing to be done more easily and economically, or if the ever increasing appreciation of

Well-maintained greenhouses covered predominately with fiberglass. This type of construction is intermediate in initial cost.

Inside a low cost polyethylene covered greenhouse which serves admirably for tropical foliage and seedling production despite the fact it is located in a near arctic climate.

The rigid, double-layered plasticized panels used to cover this greenhouse cost a good deal more than fiberglass or polyethylene. Notice the extensive use of large fans for exhausting warm air.

ornamentals by affluent societies is the driving force. Whatever the case, this industry is booming without a let up in sight.

The term "greenhouse" will be rather loosely used in this discussion. The average person in the United States likely envisions a greenhouse as being a structure covered by glass or perhaps some plastic-like material.

I believe we can continue to use this word profitably if we qualify it somewhat.

The most important qualification we must recognize is that much of what might be termed "greenhouse crop production" now takes place outside a traditional greenhouse structure. That is, production may occur in the open air or in shade structures near the greenhouse. This situation arose partially because optimum use of greenhouse space in some circumstances is accomplished if plants are stored in vertical layers in the structure at night and during inclement weather and then spread outside when weather permits. Another contributing reason is that much greenhouse production has shifted to the sunbelt states where it is possible to grow some crops, or at least some phases of crops, outdoors — often protected from the full sun by shade structures.

There are many commercial operations where it is difficult to decide whether they should be properly called greenhouses or nurseries. Perhaps the deciding factor in most people's minds is whether the majority of crop production takes place inside, as in a greenhouse, or whether it predominately takes place outdoors, such as in a nursery. Also, most people associate the word "nursery" with woody ornamental crop production. There should be no great argument with using the terms somewhat interchangeably, as long as we become more precise whenever the need arises.

GREENHOUSES ALLOW CONTROLLED PRODUCTION

The main objectives of greenhouse production are generally to grow plants out of their normal season or habitat and in a more-or-less strictly controlled environment. The degree of environmental manipulation required to meet these objectives usually means that greenhouse crop culture is a rather costly alternative to open air field production. When the proper crops are chosen for greenhouse production and suitable markets are present, the grower will hopefully realize a profit which more than compensates for the additional costs involved in this type of intensive crop culture.

The progress of agriculture and industry in the modern world has generally been brought about by newer, more controlled methods of doing things. We have found that controlling natural processes usually results in increased efficiency and a greater total amount of desired product being available than is possible by simply letting nature take its course. This intensification and control of natural processes does not result without effort. Both resources and knowledge must be applied to make it work.

Since greenhouse culture requires the most precise environmental control of any widely used means of crop production, we might assume that it requires the most intensive use of both knowledge and resources. This is, in fact, the case. The practical impact of this situation is that, on average and for an equivalent business size, more monetary resources and technology is required in the greenhouse production field than in most other aspects of horticulture.

ADVANTAGEOUS ASPECTS OF GREENHOUSE CULTURE

In return for the expenditure of considerable mental and monetary capital, the greenhouse operator expects to realize definite commercial benefits. The most obvious advantage is that a grower can produce crops out of natural season at a time when they are in high demand. Other important advantages of greenhouse production over outdoor culture are: 1) predictable as well as accelerated production schedules are possible through control of temperature or other factors; 2) physical protection of the

A beautiful crop of florist azaleas being grown in July. In earlier years, Oregon plants would be outside during the warmer months. Greenhouses provide more predictable growing conditions than can be expected outdoors.

crop from devastating climatic conditions is accomplished.

The advantages of greenhouse production over hit-or-miss open air methods intensify as our marketing opportunities become more fine-tuned and sophisticated. Often, consumers want their desires for horticultural products gratified whenever the urge hits them, not only when a product is in season. In order to satisfy the market, distributors and retailers of ornamentals must demand a steady and reliable source of supply. They do not wish to have their marketing plans upset by frost, windstorms, or drought conditions. In response to these market forces, there has been a steady trend to plant culture under cover.

Even in cases where a reasonably adequate outdoor growing program has traditionally been in place, many producers are now moving inside. A case in point is the Northwest Coast azalea production area. Years ago, production was accomplished almost entirely outdoors during seasons which were not subject to frost. Growers would take cuttings in early spring, grow plants actively through the summer, and then allow buds to condition in the cool fall weather for Christmas and Valentines Day forcing.

Since a florist-quality azalea took about two years production time, some protection was required in order to overwinter small plants intended for next year's crop, but the majority of a plant's life was spent outdoors.

Two main factors caused this time-honored production method to be altered. First, many growers decided to move under cover because the possibility of a devastating freeze in the fall as plants were being conditioned for market was unacceptable. Second, moving into greenhouses allowed growers to aim their marketing at Easter and Mothers Day market periods in addition to only earlier Christmas and Valentines selling times. Some growers now produce azaleas year-round. Moving azalea production indoors has led to a much extended selling season, and this, in turn, has resulted in an overall expansion of the azalea industry. Generally, the growers are now more profitable and more financially stable than they were under the old outdoor cultural scheme.

Incidentally, you can see that in the past azalea producers were mostly thought of as nurserymen, while at present a great number would be considered greenhouse growers.

Another fact which emerges from this example is that most horticultural growers would be well-advised to become familiar with greenhouse methods and techniques. Almost every crop requires some type of protected care during at least part of its life-cycle.

HIGH INVESTMENT REQUIRES INTENSIVE MANAGEMENT

The monetary investment required to build greenhouses varies dramatically from structure to structure, depending upon materials, labor, and the degree of environmental control necessary. If you build a bare-bones structure with your own labor and use secondhand materials, the actual cash expenses for a greenhouse may be very small. On the other hand, a brand new structure which will handle all climatic conditions year-round can be quite expensive, especially if a contractor builds the greenhouse for you.

In order to recoup your investment, a greenhouse must be intensively managed. It cannot sit half-empty when it should be full of plants, and the crops you produce must be of a high enough quality to bring a profitable price. The more you invest in a greenhouse, the more intensively it must be utilized. Greenhouse managers usually measure crop productivity in terms of how many square feet a crop occupies for a specific period of time. In the year 2000 it costs the average commercial greenhouse owner approximately $0.10 to $0.25 per square foot per week to cover operational and structure expenses only. This figure does not cover materials such as seed, soil, starter plants, or other costs directly attributable to a specific crop. Thus, a 2000 square foot greenhouse (small by industry standards) would be costing $200 to $400 per week just to keep operational. Of course, if you build an inexpensive greenhouse on surplus land and operate it yourself, the costs can be lowered a great deal.

The point is, an empty or inefficiently managed greenhouse is costing you money, not making money. Many greenhouses are constructed and managed only for spring operation. This is okay, as long as the owner builds inexpensive structures and slashes operational expenses as soon as the crop is out the door. In fact, this is one of the better operational methods for newcomers in the business to use. However, if you build an expensive greenhouse and provide heat and staff all winter, it must be filled with marketable crops.

Developing a proven, reproducible cropping and marketing program which assures a decent profit year after year should be the primary objective of every greenhouse manager. There must certainly be room in this program for introducing new varieties and methods, but these should be incorporated slowly and with adequate testing to assure they actually improve the performance of the basic program.

THE GREENHOUSE CROP PLAN

The controlled environment in greenhouses allows growers in Maine to produce more-or-less the same crops as could be grown in a Texas greenhouse. Thus, the cultural details for specific crops are fairly uniform from region to region. Why is it then, that upon visiting a number of greenhouses, one finds that each establishment has developed its own special style or method of operation?

And why will each owner or manager usually swear that their method is the right one?

You must realize that although greenhouses are intended to modify the natural climatic conditions, each increased degree of climatic modification normally involves an increase in operational cost.

Therefore, some of the restraints of the natural climate usually still apply to greenhouse production. They apply in differing degrees, depending upon the construction characteristics of each particular greenhouse.

Climate and differences in greenhouse construction are not the only causes of diversity in operational methods. Hundreds of potential crops are available for culture under greenhouse conditions. The grower must determine which crops are most profitably adapted to the particular conditions prevailing for production and marketing. There are numerous technical and economic reasons why a grower might select one crop over another: 1) the proper raw materials for good growth may or may not be economically available; 2) growers may lack enough knowledge or information; 3) certain crops may be subject to disease or insect predation; 4) one crop may require more energy input than another; 5) and on and on. The most important fact determining the crops a producer should grow is what varieties can actually be sold at a healthy profit.

Marketing possibilities vary from region to region and even from neighborhood to neighborhood, thus causing greenhouse operators to choose a variety of production scenarios, each hopefully resulting in a successful outcome for the business involved. For example, many local zoning agencies will not allow retail activity in a rural agricultural area, but they generally allow a wholesale greenhouse since it is primarily producing an agricultural crop of sorts.

Cutting or sowing Date			Open Flat	Direct Sow		Plug Flat	Crop #, Initial Pot Later Pot Size	# Finished Flats or Plants to Plant			Xtra Crops		Comments
Sched	Act	Date		Plate Size	# Times to Seed			Sched	Act	+ / –	Date Sown	# Flats	
11/8	Sow					406		Crop					
						200		Small					
							1-10" Pot	25					
							2	30					
							3	30					
							4	25					
								Total:	Total:	Total:		Total:	

Comments: Dracenas, Vinca, try some with Baucopa   Variety: 10" Pot, Begonia Non-Stop   Year:00

An example of a crop schedule. Crop schedules are essential to greenhouse production and marketing.

However variable the crop production plans are among individual greenhouses, there do arise some general patterns within the industry.

In other words, many greenhouses share a relatively common production schedule in regards to the timing and species of crops grown, while other growers concentrate their efforts upon somewhat different production schemes. These differences and similarities arise in response to the factors mentioned above which influence the decisions of individual growers. Basically, many growers make the same decisions so that we see general patterns arise among their operational plans.

A few of the more common production scenarios into which greenhouses may be classified will now be outlined. Remember, seldom would you find a facility which epitomized these descriptions perfectly, some degree of hybridization between plans is almost always the case.

Garden season only operation

This method of ornamental crop production is quite common amongst beginning and part-time growers in all sections of the country. It is also popular with more established full-time growers in climates where active gardening is practiced throughout a large part of the year. Needless to say, the crops grown are those which consumers use in their gardening endeavors.

Garden plants of all types have become big business over the last thirty years; it is this segment of the greenhouse industry which is booming the most. A voracious and generally profitable market is the main reason why so many growers gravitate toward the production of garden plants. There are, however, other reasons which influence their decision: 1) relatively inexpensive structures are necessary; 2) the manager or owner can be free other parts of the year to pursue alternative interests; 3) money is tied up only a short time in supplies and expenses; 4) the degree of technical expertise required is relatively limited.

The growing climate inside and outside the greenhouse at the time garden plants are being cropped is generally pleasant and relatively problem free. Hard to manage extremes of light and temperature associated with winter and midsummer production are avoided for the most part when an operation concentrates on garden plants.

Of course, the big draw back to this type of operation is the lack of cash flow during the remaining

Early season planting supplies and fertilizer can help start cash coming in before customers are interested in flowering plants for the garden.

Products such as pots, bulbs, seed potatoes, and soil also aid in the generation of cash flow.

part of the year. It seems a shame to build greenhouses and then shut them down after only a short period of operation.

But remember: *Our goal is profit.* If market and production conditions outside the gardening season are not amenable to a profitable operation, be happy with what you can get, and leave the money losing work to someone else. Several of the most monetarily successful and happy greenhouse owners I know have concentrated strictly upon garden plants and are content to be on vacation the rest of the year.

Most greenhouses get all the business they can handle during the spring rush, but the trick is to provide product and convince consumers to buy it a month or two on either side of the busy season. Granted, the amount of business you generate at these times may not be all that fantastic, but if the rush season covers your expenses and provides a small profit, the extra sales early and late are pure gravy. There are several strategies which can be used to increase the length of time garden plants or associated products are sold profitably.

During the preseason, you might concentrate on seeds, planting supplies, and cold-hardy plants such as pansies, violas, primroses, and perennials in general. Since there will be many gardeners at this time seeking a project

Beautiful patio planters like this can help extend the selling season in a greenhouse by at least one month.

**Petunias are hard to beat as inexpensive hanging
baskets intended for use in sunny areas.**

they can accomplish indoors, it is wise to have inexpensive
and appealing houseplants available as impulse items. Even
small tomato plants will sell reasonably well because early-
bird gardeners want to grow them even larger before the
time to plant outside arrives.

After the main busy season, full bloom hanging
baskets and patio planters sell very well if you provide a
quality product at a reasonable price. The secret to late
season sales is in growing fresh crops specifically designed
for this market period. People don't want your left over
plants from the rush season. At the very end of the season,
when you think no one would buy another plant, a half-
price sale of first rate merchandise will prolong the season

for another two or three weeks.

Although I operate my greenhouse business year-round, the spring season in 1999 accounted for 90 percent of profits. At one time, the wintertime business in ornamental plants and flowers was very good in our locale, but a severe and prolonged economic depression in the region's main industries has prompted consumers to limit their purchases of luxury items. Happily, the amount of spring business remains steady, and I have been able to modify my operation so as to take full advantage of our short gardening season. My business is still prospering while others have long since fallen prey to the poor economy.

The gardening-season-only scheme of greenhouse operation is being emphasized because it is likely to be the first step many of you take toward a career in specialized horticulture. There is a tremendous demand for garden plants in every neighborhood. Even urban dwellers are now eager buyers of plant products designed for limited space gardening. A beginner in the spring greenhouse business can easily sell a large amount of plants at retail prices even if only the basics of an intelligent marketing plan are followed. With hard work and careful advance planning, it is possible to realize a full year's profits with only a four or five month operation.

One basic problem which the spring-only grower faces is the task of finding competent employees who are willing and able to work only a few months of the year. This drawback is not usually serious for the small grower who can rely upon neighborhood housewives and afterschool teenagers to fill the gap. It is a major handicap for those who wish to expand this type of business beyond the possibilities of a small retail greenhouse. So, although a spring-only greenhouse can be very profitable as a start up enterprise, the limitation it imposes upon the development of a trained labor force for future expansion must clearly be recognized.

Combined garden season plants and holiday flowers

Most greenhouse growers get their start producing bedding plants for the gardening market. As they gain more experience, and if they want to be in the greenhouse business year-round, they begin to look for ways to utilize their greenhouses longer during the year.

A large number of these people settle into a production scheme which emphasizes garden plants during the main season and then switches to flowering pot plants from fall through midwinter. Poinsettias for Christmas are usually the main money making flower crop in this type of operation, but Thanksgiving, Valentines Day, and Easter, in increasing order of importance, can also be relied upon to provide a market for potted flowers. At Mother's Day, which is perhaps the largest flower occasion of the year, growers are faced with the conflict between space needed by spring garden crops and space for potted flowers.

A cropping scheme like this can significantly increase income, and also allow key employees to remain at work all year. The drawbacks are that better structures are needed for winter protection, and a higher and more varied knowledge on the part of the grower is required. In addition, most growers have a hard time selling all the potted flowers they grow at retail price. They must usually sell a large proportion of these flowers at wholesale to flower shops and mass outlets. Thus, except in the best circumstances, winter flower production is seldom as profitable as is spring garden plant production. Furthermore, in contrast to the vigorous growth plants exhibit in the spring, winter culture is sometimes difficult with large amounts of heat usually being needed to force plants along. I do not wish to discourage anyone by my cautionary statements from planning a year-round commercial greenhouse. But it must be pointed out that this is a more complex and risky venture than is an in and out spring-only operation. If you expect to expand beyond the limitations of a small neighborhood greenhouse, it is almost obligatory that you progress beyond growing strictly retail spring crops.

Continuous foliage plant and potted flower production

Although the garden plant market is generally the most profitable aspect of greenhouse production, some growers find that, over the long run, a cultural scheme which leads to a steady flow of plant production throughout the year is best suited to their facilities, markets, and personal inclination. This objective is often accomplished by specializing in indoor foliage plants and decorative potted flowers. Individual greenhouses may specialize in only foliage, only potted flowers, or both at the same time.

If you have a large retail outlet or multiple outlets, it is possible to market a good deal of foliage and flowers by this means. However, most growers in this production scheme find that they cannot move a large enough volume through their own retail efforts to support a year-round growing operation. They must then look to other florists and mass outlets as buyers for their excess production.

Some greenhouses, either from the start or in step-by-step progression, become totally oriented toward wholesale production of foliage, potted flowers, or both. Needless to say, the wholesale operation must be of considerable size to generate enough volume so that adequate total profit is realized. Wholesale profit margins simply do not lead to a good income picture unless large amounts of merchandise is sold. This is the basic premise of the wholesale trade: large volume at low price.

Beginners in the greenhouse business must not allow themselves to be drawn into impossible situations. A small neighborhood greenhouse operated solely by the owner cannot produce enough plants economically to compete in the wholesale arena unless special circumstances apply. Yes, it may be possible to sell all that you produce at a fair market price, but unless you grow a large volume of plants efficiently, the wholesale price you receive may not cover production expenses. Small greenhouses must generally operate on retail terms to be successful.

The statements just made about wholesale businesses are based solely upon strict accounting procedures. It may well be that if every expense is not accounted for, you will find yourself ahead monetarily every year. That is to say, if you do not charge the cost of land, taxes, minor utilities, some family labor, and miscellaneous expenses against the business, it may appear that a profit is being made. This is a common mistake of people whose personal assets are unavoidably mixed with a business operation: they let the business use their personal assets for free. The only way to see if a true business profit is being made is to charge the business for all materials

Specialization in plant products not widely available from other sources is a proven route to success in the greenhouse industry.

and services you provide it.

A steady, repetitive cropping system throughout the year and from year to year allows growers to plan production and marketing carefully and fine-tune their efficiency. If you must seek outside financing, this is a type of predictable and stable situation which loan officials will look upon most favorably — even if it may not yield the greatest profits. Furthermore, some growers prefer the reduced anxiety and risk levels which result from a repetitive crop schedule.

Of course, if you can't sell all production at retail, then there is the problem of contacting and convincing other retail outlets to handle your plants and flowers. This is not usually an easy task in the beginning, but, fortunately, it becomes almost automatic after accounts have been established. Most shops will reorder time after time for years and years simply out of habit, as long as you provide good merchandise and service at a fair price.

The best way to get established in a steady flower and foliage production scheme is to ease into it gradually over several years. Seldom will a grower have enough technical and marketing expertise to start a profitable year-round operation from scratch. Most likely, you will want to start a seasonal spring operation, then graduate to producing a few holiday potted flowers in conjunction with the spring plants, and then (if it seems advisable) begin aiming at specializing in year-round flowers and foliage.

Single crop specialist

As a grower becomes established in a greenhouse operation, it sometimes becomes apparent that the most satisfactory course for future expansion lies in producing a specialized single crop. The factors causing this situation may vary, but, in many cases, it results from a consuming interest which the grower develops in a particular group of plants. Other major factors can be market conditions and local climatic suitability.

This type of operation usually sells crops on the wholesale market, and, as a result, must be of sufficient size to produce enough volume for satisfactory profits. Sometimes, the specialized plants being grown require extraordinary facilities and technical knowledge; this fact may protect the grower from widespread competition and allow for a highly profitable situation even with a limited volume of crops. The latter situation does not occur often or endure for extended periods of time because it is usually only a matter of time before the necessary knowledge becomes widespread. Basing a business upon a single product allows for the concentration of energy and capital in a very efficient manner. However, this is a double-edged sword. A single product company is vulnerable to factors which make the product obsolete.

A perfect example of this situation is the carnation industry in Colorado. Until the 1950's, Colorado was the carnation capital of America, but, as jet cargo became both efficient and reliable, cut flowers could be economically shipped from continent to continent. Because the higher altitudes of Columbia, South America were even more suitable to carnations than was Colorado, and because labor was cheaper in Columbia, large carnation growers established production facilities there, and Colorado was eclipsed as a major force in carnation production. Most Colorado carnation growers went broke or switched to other crops.

There are several crops in which growers seem to have specialized for one reason or another. The driving forces are complex and not appropriate for investigation in an introductory book, but the fact is that specialization is one of the proven routes to success in the greenhouse industry. Growers of azaleas, cacti, bromeliads, bonsai trees, roses, and several other major and minor crops are, more often than not, specialists in only that crop.

If you possess specialized knowledge about a group of economically valuable or potentially valuable ornamental plants, it may well be that a specialized greenhouse operation would suit you fine. More than one individual has become rich and famous by developing their interest in a particular group of plants into a successful business enterprise. But, here again, a marketing plan must be developed to go along with your horticultural knowledge.

Starter plant specialist

In the early stages of life, plants, like humans, are in special need of intensive and constant care. Whether they receive adequate nurture during juvenile stages often determines their productivity as adult specimens. This intensive care is best accomplished in special facilities where a higher level of supervision and technical knowledge is available.

Many experienced greenhouse growers who possess the resources (both mentally and monetarily) to provide intensive care conditions have specialized as producers of starter plants for the rest of the industry. Often these growers will be engaged in developing new varieties for which they obtain governmental patents. As the owner of a patented variety, you are allowed by law to control the reproduction of the variety in question. You may restrict propagation to your own facilities or license other growers to reproduce the plants, for which they pay a royalty fee.

The more successful propagation specialists are often considered the leaders in the industry since a large number of unspecialized and smaller growers are dependent upon the specialists as a source for healthy starter plants and for cultural information. Many propagation specialists amass considerable wealth since other growers are willing to pay a handsome price in order to avoid the headaches of starting their own plants.

If a specialist happens to develop and patent a particularly popular variety, it can be the horticultural equivalent of writing a best selling book or producing an academy award winning movie. A plant patent lasts for many years, and even a modestly successful variety may be the source of considerable royalty income over an extended period of time.

Only a small number of propagation specialists ever attain "star" status, but many become regional or local suppliers of starter plants of one or several varieties. Plant propagation is a process in which success depends heavily upon the practitioner's strict attention to detail and cleanliness. Anyone who is not disposed towards these attributes should forget about becoming a starter plant specialist.

Cut flower specialist

Cut flowers were, at one time, probably the major crop in most greenhouses all across America. Now they are of major importance only in specific areas and with a limited number of growers. Although their numbers have decreased, the average size of cut flower greenhouse ranges and the total production of cut flowers has increased. This change has been brought about by the general tendency of business in America toward specialization and by changes in the transportation system.

Because they have been detached from the root ball, cut flowers are rather light in weight when compared to most other ornamental crops. Furthermore, because in most varieties the blooms can be laid flat on top of one another without significant damage, cut flowers are easily and economically shipped by air. As air freight services became dependable, widespread, and cheap, it was more economical for cut flowers to be grown in areas where the climate was near ideal and the labor cheap. The majority of cut flowers in the United States are now grown in California and Florida. A good deal of total production in some varieties is grown outside under field conditions. As was mentioned earlier, because air transport has become so economical, much of the cut flowers in the United States are now produced overseas. Columbia, the Netherlands, Spain, Israel, and Australia are major suppliers.

The situation in cut flowers today does not lend itself to easy entry by small, diversified growers. There are, however, isolated possibilities for local greenhouses to supply cut flowers under specific conditions. Some smaller growers concentrate upon varieties which can be shipped only with difficulty. Snapdragons and delphiniums are a case in point. The blooms do not pack well, and, in addition, quality flowers of these varieties are not easily grown under the warm weather conditions usually prevailing in the major cut flower growing regions. There are several minor cut flower crops in which the same or similar conditions prevail. So, if you are a cut flower enthusiast, take heart, there is still room for you in the greenhouse industry, but the crops and markets must be chosen carefully to make a profit.

GREENHOUSES NOT SELF-SUFFICIENT

No matter what type of cropping system your greenhouse may emphasize or where it is located, you will usually be dependent upon other greenhouses to supply some of your plant or flower needs. Seldom is a greenhouse 100% self-sufficient as far as plant needs are concerned. Most purchase a fair amount of seedlings and rooted cuttings from specialists, and some buy in a good amount of finished flowers and plants to round out their inventory.

There is nothing wrong with this situation as long as it is part of a well thought out production and marketing plan, rather than resulting from laziness or a fear of overcoming specific crop culture problems. In fact, some greenhouse owners, after careful thought, find that buying most of their plants and merely using their greenhouse as an inventory holding area is the most efficient and profitable method of operation. This latter situation is not much different than being a strictly retail outlet, except that a larger backup of inventory is held in stock.

No one can prescribe how much plant material you should buy from other sources. It depends upon the prices and the selection available, how good a grower you are, transport factors, and many other variables. It depends mostly upon the marketing and cultural plan you have devised. It is very easy to get "addicted" to letting other suppliers do the most difficult part of your work — one must constantly make sure the purchase of outside plant material is justified.

Under most circumstances, I favor being as independent as possible from outside suppliers of plant materials. In this way, you develop a completely integrated cultural and marketing system which minimizes the probability of disruptions in your supply line. An example of the problems you can get into by relying upon other growers is the common practice of buying geranium cuttings from outside sources for the spring crop. If the supplying grower does not ship your cuttings or sends them a month late, the peak selling season is missed for one of your most important crops. Believe me, this scenario is not rare!

Another big reason for remaining relatively independent is the difficulty a lot of small growers have getting plant material delivered safely and economically to their location. Besides, doesn't it seem as if you could

Inside a greenhouse of the type and approximate size specified for our cost analysis presented in this text. Low cost but very sturdy and modern.

Well maintained greenhouses covered predominately with fiberglass. This type of production is intermediate in initial cost.

The rigid, double layer plasticized panels used to cover this greenhouse cost a good deal more than fiberglass or polyethylene. This house was first covered 50 years ago with glass. Notice the extensive use of large fans used for exhausting warm air.

raise the product at a slightly higher cost than the other grower and then pocket at least some of the freight money? Producing your own small plants also reduces the importation of exotic insects and diseases from other areas.

There are certainly times and situations when you should buy in plant material, but weigh the alternatives carefully. The expenses mount up quickly and suck most of the profit out of your operation. Isolated small town growers must be especially willing to remain self-sufficient.

A great deal of improvement and innovation has taken place in the last ten years regarding production, quality control, and shipping of small starter plants. There

Table 3

Qualifying statements which apply to tables 4 and 5 of the greenhouse economic model which follows.

A. Greenhouse structure is of new material and adequately equipped to operate in spring or fall of a moderately cold climate.

B. Owner supplies labor to build greenhouse except for a few specific tasks, such as electrical hookups and occasional hourly labor hired.

C. Owner supplies land and utility access.

D. Greenhouse structure is an engineered steel frame, double-inflated plastic kit available from manufacturers and is of modern design with automatic heat, cooling fans, and inflation blowers.

E. Owner devotes approximately 1000 hours per year to growing and selling spring crop, making repairs, record keeping, and planning.

F. Model assumes one complete crop of standard spring bedding plants in flats, each flat occupying 1.5 square feet and containing 12 packs of 6 plants each. This equals a total of 2,000 flats each year.

G. Hanging baskets overhead in greenhouse will replace the value of any bedding flats accounted for in model but not actually grown because some space is necessary for aisles.

H. With a 3% dumpage rate, the number of flats available for sale is reduced to 1,940 per year.

I. Retail price of $23.88 per flat is the actual price obtained by author's retail department in 1999. This is higher than average chain store prices but lower than some independent garden center prices.

J. Assume plants will be sold at retail greenhouse. If alternative lot space in high traffic area is rented for retail sales, the $2388 budgeted for advertising would be used for spring season rental.

K. Building and related equipment costs are taken from actual 1999 catalog prices while miscellaneous construction costs are estimated from author's experience. Fixed greenhouse operation costs are estimated from author's experience while variable costs per unit are taken from the author's own production cost records in a commercial greenhouse.

Table 4

Expenses involved in operating a 3,000 square foot commercial greenhouse for the spring gardening season only. These costs can be lowered by using recycled pots, used equipment, and doing more work yourself.

Building and equipment costs—assume new steel frame prefabricated greenhouse kit is purchased.

Greenhouse kit with frame, endwalls, doors $4300
Heater, ventilation fan, water lines, and utility hookups 3700
Ground preparation for concrete posts 700
Wheel barrow, pump, soil mixer, miscellaneous equipment.
     Used condition if possible...1500
Total building and equipment costs.. $10,200
Yearly building and equipment cost if total is amortized
     at 10% interest over a 15 year usable lifespan $1315.44

Variable product costs per unit of plants produced

Containers for plants $0.30
Flats—used only 1 year 0.40
Soil 0.30
Seed and germination materials 1.50
Total variable cost per unit (flat) $2.50

Fixed greenhouse operation costs per year

Yearly cost for double-layer polyethylene covering on
     greenhouse if replaced 4 times in a 15 year period $133
Insurance 600
Water 500
Heating fuel 1300
Electricity 300
Fertilizer 250
Pest control 300
Maintenance and repair materials 600
Taxes, property 400
Miscellaneous expenses 700
Total fixed operating costs $5083

Table 5

Revenues, costs, and profits for operating a 3,000 square foot greenhouse in spring gardening season only. Refer to table 3 for qualifying statement.

Calculation of yearly revenues

Greenhouse produces 1 spring crop for a total of 2,000 flats.
Multiply this by a retail selling price of $23.88 per
flat to arrive at total gross revenues $47,760

Calculation of yearly selling and production costs

Cost of advertising or high traffic sales lot rental to
reach customers, assume 5% of gross revenues
(0.05 x $47,760) $2388
Extra sales help in busiest month at $7 per hour 1200
Deduct for 3% crop spoilage (0.03 x 47,760) 1432.80
Variable cost of planting 2,000 flats of plants at $2.50 each 5000
Fixed operating costs per year from Table 4 5083
Building and equipment costs per year from Table 4.................<u>1315.44</u>
Total costs per year for selling and production $16,419.24

Calculation of before tax profits

**Total retail revenues less total production and selling
costs ($47,760.00 - $16,419.24) $31,340.76**

are some very good products at reasonable prices offered by reliable suppliers. This situation is getting better all of the time. I evaluate my operation each year to see if I can take advantage of good opportunities to buy plants, rather than produce them on-site. However, due to our isolated location, knowledgeable staff and management, and unusual needs for precision scheduling, it is almost always more profitable to grow our plants from step one. Most greenhouses would likely be better off purchasing more starter plants than I do.

EXAMPLE OF GREENHOUSE
EXPENSE AND PROFITS

Although each greenhouse operation will have a somewhat different economic picture, I think it will be beneficial to examine a specific example in detail. This will not only give you actual figures for a common cropping scheme, but it will also familiarize you with a method by which other greenhouse crops can be analyzed. The method could also be used, with minor modifications, for examining the economics involved with other horticultural business enterprises which will be described later in this book.

The example presented involves a small greenhouse of 3000 square feet which is to be operated only in the spring. This situation is portrayed because it is a fairly common size greenhouse and cropping scheme for a newcomer in the industry to select. Normally, this size greenhouse will not produce adequate income to support a family, but it is a good size to start out with part-time the first year. I would estimate that about 9000 square feet of greenhouse space is necessary to realize a good family income if the operation sells its produce mainly at retail, and most labor is provided by family members. There are several qualifications we must place upon the example to be examined in order to interpret it accurately. The qualifications are presented in Table 3.

The descriptive terms and numerical data given in Tables 3, 4, and 5 will require a few minutes of study in order to completely understand them. I am attempting to accurately show you how much it would cost to build and operate a greenhouse through the spring gardening season. When all expenses are subtracted from the gross revenues (sales), we arrive at a before tax profit.

There are several points which may require some clarification. First, the profit figure represents what you could expect for devoting approximately 1/2 of a normal work year to the greenhouse enterprise.

A 40 hour work week equals 2080 hours a year, while our example requires you to put in only 1000 hours. Of course, if you chose to, you could have someone else do most of this work. You should double the profit figure to arrive at a fair estimate of how much you would make if you devoted full-time to the greenhouse.

The greenhouse structure should have a usable life-span of at least 15 years. Only the annual mortgage payment (taken from bank mortgage tables) necessary to pay off the greenhouse completely in 15 years is added to the yearly expenses. The entire greenhouse cost cannot be attributed to a single year; it must be spread out evenly over its 15 year life-span.

The term "flats" in our example may be unfamiliar to some readers. It is a trade term which means the outer tray into which growing containers are placed. We have based our example calculations upon plants being grown only in this type of container. In reality, you would likely grow in several different container sizes and types, but the price you would receive per square foot occupied would at least equal the price received per square foot occupied by flats. In my experience, the relative retail price of plants in flats is less than plants in other size containers. I have only made this simplification to make the example more easily understood.

The $31340.76 profit figure for halftime work may not impress some of you who already make a lot of money, but it is a significant income for many people. You also have the option (for very little extra construction expense) of equipping the greenhouse to produce crops all year. You should also realize that if you expand your operation to 4 or 5 or even 10 of these greenhouses, you could easily manage them yourself with a few lower level employees.

I expect the price I receive for my plants (which is used in the example) can at least be matched by other growers. My prices are on the upper end but certainly not the highest in town. Many growers have told me that they could not possibly get the price I have quoted, but I have been doing it year after year for over a quarter of a century. Some people set their prices even higher. Total income can be increased by selling such things as seed, fertilizers, potting soil and other related products which complement greenhouse plants.

Incidentally, the profit figure shown in this edition of "Make Money" is $3970.20 higher than the figure reported 8 years ago in the first edition. I have raised prices for plants approximately 18% during this period to account for inflation. For year 2000 I plan a large increase of 25% to compensate for our continuing stress upon high quality.

Two alternative scenarios should be investigated at this time. First, suppose you construct an all-weather, top-of-the-line greenhouse for twice the money projected in our model. You can see that twice the yearly building and equipment cost would only take $1315.44 off your yearly profits. This points out that the initial cost of greenhouses is not the critical factor in success or failure — that is, if you can afford the increased cost at the start. Second, pretend that you sell all your plants at wholesale for 1/2 the retail figure we used. It is easy to see that profits would decrease tremendously; you make a little money, but your volume sold would have to go up perhaps 10 times to make a decent profit. **Pricing is the critical factor to success**. This point will be emphasized several times later on.

Another point that needs to be mentioned is the relatively small cost of getting into a horticultural business. I often see franchise opportunities for fast food, etc. advertised in *The Wall Street Journal* that require $200,000 to $500,000 just to start a single store (this probably doesn't cover the total value of land and building). Compare this cost with the figure illustrated in Table 4.

Many of you are probably thinking now that you would like to get in a greenhouse business but cannot see any way to come up with the $15,000 to $20,000 investment necessary to build and operate the greenhouse used in the example. This concern will be addressed in a later chapter. There are many financing alternatives possible, especially if you own a piece of land or a home. The easiest way to cut start up costs is by building your own greenhouse from scrap materials and by cutting a few corners with equipment, heaters, and other materials.

These elementary figures demonstrate that there are good financial opportunities in the horticultural field. The satisfaction of being your own boss and the healthy mix of mental and physical work are added psychological benefits you may enjoy. Growing and selling plants is a very secure occupation. As the pressures of modern living increase, more people turn to decorating with plants indoors and gardening to alleviate their tensions. The trend towards urbanized societies means these pressures will grow even more and, thus, ensure a healthy market for plants and flowers in the future.

Most of the really successful greenhouse owners I know started their enterprise as a sideline while they worked at regular jobs. After a year or two of learning the ropes and developing a clientele, they usually saw their businesses take off at an astounding rate. There are numerous extremely large greenhouse firms started only a few years ago by individuals like you. The horticultural industry is truly in a boom era and will stay that way as long as the trends of the last thirty years continue. Sales of foliage plants, potted flowers, and bedding plants have increased greatly in recent years. There is plenty of room for newcomers in this expanding market.

Lots of people have plenty of money and prefer top-of-the-line merchandise. Discount store plants simply don't meet these consumer's expectations in most cases. Why don't you offer them ones that do?

OUTLOOK FOR THE GREENHOUSE INDUSTRY

In addition to the generally rosy economic outlook for greenhouse products, there are some specific points which relate fundamentally to the greenhouse physical environment.

Climate inside the greenhouse can be altered so that a particular crop may be grown under ideal conditions in almost any geographical setting.

This situation assures that new or improved ornamental plant varieties can and will be grown in any region of the world where profitable consumer markets exist. Development of these new varieties in response to market demand will lead to a continual stream of new ornamental plant products. This is a very healthy condition for the greenhouse industry. We have new and exciting products each year to help expand sales.

The greenhouse climate also assures that we have a drawing card to attract production workers at reasonable wages. Other industries and other segments of the horticultural industry are not so lucky. A large number of people consider greenhouse work to be a pleasant indoor job. The same cannot be said for an outdoor ornamental nursery where plants are many times larger and weather often unfavorable. So, the greenhouse industry has an inside track on one of the most important problems facing American business: how to attract and hold competent workers at reasonable prices.

The explosion of technical knowledge in the greenhouse field has only just begun and indicates that we may expect the culture of ornamentals under cover to continue expanding significantly for many years.

Personal Note from The Author:

A considerable number of people who I have counseled about starting a horticultural business question whether there is still good opportunity in the industry. They respond to my enthusiasm by saying that "everything was easier in the old days" — few government regulations, less cut throat competition, better employees, etc..

Yes, some things were easier to deal with then, but, on the whole, there is more opportunity now than previously. We have a greatly expanded market, tons of beautiful new plant varieties, more good machines to do the hard work, and infinitely more information to help us do a good job.

Older growers had to build knowledge through long apprenticeship or through costly trial and error. You have the advantage of quickly learning both the basics and details through the numerous books myself and others have provided. In addition, there are many videos, tradeshows, company customer service departments, and educational facilities that did not exist 25 years ago.

The problems and opportunities are still there, although somewhat different. Overall, this industry is even greater and more rewarding than in earlier years.

Chapter 5

PRODUCTION AND MARKETING OF ORNAMENTAL NURSERY PLANTS GROWN OUTDOORS

The distinction which is made here between greenhouse grown and outdoor grown ornamentals is not entirely satisfactory since there are all sorts of situations where the dividing line becomes fuzzy. Some plants are grown indoors for awhile and then finished outside, or certain crops may be moved in and out, depending upon the weather. Certain varieties, such as Palms and Hibiscus, may be considered outdoor nursery plants in Florida, while in Minnesota they must be grown indoors. Such a distinction generally has some usefulness and I hope you will be helped more than you are confused by this method of presentation.

In the previous chapter, we listed several advantages of greenhouse culture over outdoor crop production. Therefore, this topic need not be explored in further detail. It will be enough to emphasize again that the chief reasons most production still occurs outside is that it is more economical for most varieties during the majority of their life cycle. An open field is less expensive to own and operate than is a greenhouse.

Anyone who has time, knowledge, and a piece of ground can get started in the business of producing ornamental plants outdoors. A lack of capital and other amenities may limit the types and amounts of nursery stock you can grow, but it does not prevent you from getting established in one form or another. Even if you don't own any land, it is almost always possible to rent or lease a small parcel on very reasonable terms.

Many species of common nursery plants can be reproduced from seed, cuttings, or divisions which are free for the gathering in your immediate neighborhood. Getting started in the business needn't involve purchasing a lot of expensive starter plants from other growers. Buying plants helps avoid the time-consuming process of starting from scratch, and it enables you to handle a broader line of merchandise, but it runs costs up considerably. You must decide whether it is advisable to start most small plants or buy them. If you have the resources, it will likely prove most effective to buy all the varieties except those which are easiest to start. Many of the newer tree varieties are propagated by grafting techniques which are not economical for smaller growers to practice.

Trees and shrubs generally are the focal point of the urban landscape. Therefore, most consumers are willing to spend more money on these types of plants than they are on other horticultural crops. For this reason, and also because flowers and perennials are covered in preceding and following chapters, we will now deal with woody plants.

Typical outdoor shade structure used to offer some protection for nursery crops. Can be used as a selling area, as in this photograph, or as a nursery area for newly potted stock.

MANAGE NURSERY OPERATIONS EFFECTIVELY

It may appear that since nursery land is relatively cheap when compared to a greenhouse structure, the manager or owner of an outdoor nursery could enjoy a somewhat more relaxed approach towards business. This is true to a certain extent, but, in some respects, the nurserymen's life is more difficult because outdoor crops are subject to many perils not present in the controlled greenhouse climate. Furthermore, the most difficult job — that of selling a crop profitably — is no less a challenge to the outdoor producer.

Cold frame tunnels used to protect shrubs from extreme cold. Note the open ends on the structures. Too much heat in winter can quickly kill plants.

Although the outdoor ornamental grower may have less initial monetary investment to lose in case of business failure, the enterprise must still be managed intensively and effectively in order to develop a profitable operation. Just because there is little risk of losing a great deal of money, doesn't mean that profits will magically appear. It is sometimes harder for people to maintain the necessary degree of vigilance and motivation if they are not subject to a high risk level.

Each step of a nursery growing operation must be carefully coordinated with a definite marketing program before you set out the first row of trees or shrubs. The most serious mistake a nursery grower is liable to make is that of growing crops helter-skelter without a timetable, cultural plan, or a well-conceived means of selling the crop. Remember, you are in business, not dabbling at a hobby!

John's Hillside Nursery

These hardy perennials have been grown outside all winter. They can be planted directly into the ground now. We recommend covering only if the temperature drops below 25 degrees. Enjoy!!

Informational signs which let customers know about the benefits of buying locally produced plants will help you sell crops at top prices.

NURSERY OWNERS MUST BE PATIENT

Traditionally, nursery owners have measured crop cycles in years rather than weeks or months. This type of schedule does not suit people who expect immediate results. Although the amount of time required to raise some types of nursery crops has been reduced through new growing methods, you must still be of a patient nature to thrive in this business.

The often slow growth progress of nursery crops means that plans must be made carefully to make sure your culture and marketing plan results in the desired outcome after several years have been invested in a crop.

Inventory turnover in some types of nursery operations can be very slow in the early years of business.

If you specialize in larger specimen trees of slower growing varieties, it could be five years or more before the first crop of saleable trees is harvested. An operation that is planned around varieties and plant sizes which offer a relatively quick inventory turnover will result in cash flow beginning the first year.

NURSERY PLANTS AND CLIMATES

Outdoor nursery production is primarily controlled by climatic conditions which exist at the site. Selling of crops is also dependent upon weather to a large degree. The unique character of each local climate, even from town to town, can work to the benefit or detriment of nursery operations. Without careful planning, you will reap most of the disadvantages while gathering few of the benefits.

The plant varieties selected for cultivation and almost every aspect of their subsequent growth will in some way be dependent upon climatic conditions. Even the influence of ancient climates will be reflected in the materials composing field soils. Nursery managers must learn to accept the limits which climate places upon them; you can not do battle with such powerful forces and expect to win. Of course, there are some small tricks of the trade which can help overcome minor climatic hurdles, but, by and large, your business is at the mercy of Mother Nature. Learn to live with Her.

On the other side of the coin, climatic variability provides an opportunity for the smaller retail grower to attract and hold customers through his or her intimate knowledge of how to grow landscape plants successfully in the local area. This advantage may not be of great importance for larger wholesale growers who depend upon far away clients to purchase most of their product, but it is the key element for success in the type of local retail nursery most readers of this book are likely to start.

Thus, one of the major disadvantages of outdoor crop culture can actually be turned into a competitive edge by those nursery people who exploit it fully. You must let customers know at every turn the benefits of purchasing trees and shrubs produced locally by a person who understands the cultural methods necessary for successful landscaping at their home or business. In fact, your knowledge should be the main commodity of business, with the plant material producing the initial point of contact between you and the customer. Furthermore, you must be sure to set prices at levels which will adequately compensate for the valuable knowledge provided to customers.

Growers will always be faced with the challenge of discount stores selling nursery stock at prices which often do not even equal normal production costs. There is no way the independent nursery can compete price-wise; you must build a business upon knowledgeable advice and high levels of service to that segment of the consumer market which is willing to pay for what you offer. Apparently, most people still prefer to purchase their landscape plants from independent operators. Every reputable market survey released to this date shows that independent nurseries and garden centers remain the first choice of consumers for purchases of plant material.

Since climate affects nursery crop culture so dramatically, it is hardly surprising that finding books which outline the particular varieties are hard to find and seldom provide accurate information about growing under all conditions which are likely to be encountered. It would be next to impossible for an author to deal with the thousands of nursery varieties popular in various sections of the United States, much less to provide cultural guides for production of each one under the varying climatic and soil conditions which might be present. This fact makes it somewhat more difficult for beginning nursery growers, but it makes their accumulated knowledge even more valuable in the future.

COMBINATION OF NURSERY AND LANDSCAPE BUSINESS

A complete landscaping and plant installation service is a logical extension of the specialized retail services you should offer at the nursery sales lot. In some cases, nursery owners have found that the landscaping service is a more lucrative business proposition than is selling plants. Although a landscaping enterprise can be profitable in and of itself, the more successful ones are usually an offshoot of a nursery operation. Undoubtedly this is the case because being in a nursery business allows you to more easily carry a large inventory of plants for landscaping jobs and helps in making contact with potential customers. Clients who see an established nursery business in operation will feel more assured that the landscape job is guaranteed by a substantial firm. There are several good computer programs available for helping landscapers design, price, and install jobs. Many state nursery and landscape associations also publish manuals and provide educational programs to help their members provide top-notch professional services.

FIELD AND CONTAINER NURSERIES

Until after World War II, almost every nursery was a field operation which resembled a typical farm. The nurseries might be generally smaller and more intensively worked than were fields of agricultural crops, but the basic operation was similar. Nursery stock was sold as bareroot material for immediate planting in the customer's yard or sometimes, especially with evergreens, as balled and burlapped stock which allowed customers some leeway as to when the plant could be placed in the landscape. The planting season was limited to the cooler times of the year when plants could stand the shock of being transplanted.

This was an unfavorable situation for both the nursery owner and customers. The nursery owner wanted a method of production and marketing which would allow for a longer selling season and for less concentration of production activities in the spring months. Customers hoped for some means of being able to enjoy planting through the summer and seeing their trees and shrubs leafed out and growing before placing them in the ground.

It is surprising that the nursery industry took so long to come up with the concept of containerized nursery stock. Sure, there were isolated growers who used this method of operation in earlier years, but only since the 1950's has the containerized plant become the almost universally accepted means of offering nursery stock for sale at the retail level. Many producers have gone a step further by growing their plants in containers from start to finish. The container revolution has allowed nursery stock to be effectively marketed by mass merchandisers but it has also made it possible for independent retailers to actively sell healthy plants through most of the year, thus greatly increasing their cash flow.

The field nursery

The preference of retail nursery outlets for containerized plant material might lead you to believe that most plants are now grown in containers. This is not the case. Field grown nursery stock still accounts for the majority of production; the major change being not in how the plants are grown but in how they are marketed to the final customer. Today, most of the smaller trees and shrubs grown in fields are destined to be planted in containers before being sold at retail. Most larger field grown trees are still sold as balled and burlapped stock, but there is, even here, some trend toward containerization.

Field growing has, to a large extent, ceased to be a major activity at most retail nurseries. The smaller retail nursery owner usually finds that is more efficient to purchase the lion's share of plant material to be containerized from wholesale specialists. Many retail operations still maintain a limited field area for growing specialty crops which they consider economical or which they cannot easily find elsewhere.

It should be emphasized now that planting bareroot and balled and burlapped nursery stock is still a frequent practice — especially when consumers purchase from an independent nursery or landscaper. Not all trees and shrubs are sold in containers. In fact, since recent research has shown that improperly treated container plants sometimes produce poor results in the landscape, there has been more interest in bareroot planting (it also saves on cost). Emphasizing bareroot planting is one way independent retailers can lower the cost for customers and still provide excellent material. Conditions, however, must be favorable for this type of plant material: 1) retailers need a cool, damp

storage area to keep bareroot stock dormant; 2) stock should
be planted before hot, dry summer conditions arrive.

Although the field grown nursery business is
dominated by a relatively few large wholesale growers,
there is room in this segment of the industry for new smaller
growers who limit their activities to specialized high value
crops and who supply landscapers and retail consumers
with the convenience of locally grown material.

Recent advances in container design have allowed
producers to introduce several variations in growing
procedures. For example, some plants are grown in normal
field conditions but with the roots placed in semi-restrictive
fabric bags before planting. Hopefully, this practice allows
plants to grow more freely in the field than in solid-wall
containers but also restricts roots closer to the plant so that
a greater root mass may be harvested easily.

Most of the new techniques are employed with the
idea that the advantages of both field and container growing
may somehow be incorporated into a single system.

The container nursery

There are two general ways of operating a container
growing operation for trees and shrubs. Either you buy
bareroot or balled and burlapped stock from a specialist,
and pot it up shortly before sale, or you actually grow the
plant in containers for an extended period. A small retail
nursery seldom becomes involved in the latter method.
Growing plants in containers for an extended period is
usually done by larger or more specialized wholesale
nurseries.

The typical nursery operation the readers of this
book would be advised to start is a short-term container

A bareroot dormant plant trimmed and labeled properly before being containerized.

nursery. This means that you buy bareroot deciduous (trees and shrubs that lose their leaves in fall) stock in a dormant condition and pot it to selling containers anywhere from one to six months before sale. The plants are allowed to root and produce leaves before they are sold to retail consumers.

There is a good deal of variation in how far ahead different nursery people pot their dormant plants up, but it is obvious that the longer the plants are in the pot (within reason), the more established and better quality they are. Evergreens are not often potted completely bareroot, but many short-term container growers use evergreens with a

A bareroot dormant rose plant shortly after being potted in a biodegradable woodfiber container. Certain varieties look and perform better in a container program.

minimum size soil ball for this purpose. Using a plant with a small soil ball is less expensive than potting with a much larger soil ball and comparable quality can be delivered to the customer if plants are allowed to become established in the container for a sufficient amount of time.

Numerous retail nurseries never pot their own stock or may only plant certain varieties. They purchase recently potted stock from growers who specialize in potting to containers. By following this route, you may sometimes eliminate the risk that unhealthy plants fail to bud out properly, and sometimes the grower will allow you to hand

The beautiful result of expert care only nine weeks after potting. Rose plants like this sell in volume at top prices. Your growing expertise and variety selection can make the difference between success and failure.

pick stock so that the nicer specimens may be chosen.

Various states have laws which regulate the types of pots which may be used for short-term container nursery stock, and laws may also specify the amount of time plants must be in the pots before sale. When getting started in this type of business operation, you should visit with the local county extension agent or the appropriate division in the state department of agriculture in order to be aware of any regulations which apply.

Apple trees which have recently been containerized from dormant bareroot stock. No protection is usually given to trees and shrubs potted in this manner if plants are sufficiently dormant when potted.

Local climatic conditions will dictate the exact methods used to establish container nursery stock. In many of the more humid and moderate climatic regions, little initial or subsequent care is required because extremely hard freezes and violent, dry windstorms are not common during late winter or early spring when most operators pot up their plants. Wet snows and good rainfall at this time also limit the amount of additional irrigation needed. In harsh climates, like the Rocky Mountains or Desert Southwest, it may be necessary to provide a good deal of care after potting to ensure survival.

Evergreens dug with a soil ball and then containerized for sale in woodfiber pots. These plants are easier to care for on the sales lot and easier to move to the customer's location than if left strictly in ball and burlap.

As more and more containerized nursery stock was utilized, it became obvious that, in certain circumstances, this system of handling plants was detrimental to their future health. Research soon showed that plants which were grown in containers too long developed long roots which circled the inside walls of the containers. Eventually, this phenomenon can produce a strangled mass of roots which never grow normally into new soil when planted in the landscape.

There is much more to this story than can be detailed in this introductory book, but this example should point out that the obvious benefits of containerized nursery stock must be balanced with other not so obvious problems. A good deal more information about how to treat nursery stock can be found in *The Greenhouse and Nursery Handbook.*

NURSERY STOCK MARKETING

In most sections of the United States, nursery plant sales take place predominately in the spring months. With the introduction of high quality and readily available containerized stock, there has been a trend toward more summer and fall planting. However, consumers are still not especially enthusiastic toward planting at these times. Landscapers are a different story. They simply cannot install all of their plants in one or two spring months so they are generally active from the time the frost leaves the ground until it freezes solid late in the fall. Part of the explosion in landscaping business is due to the ready availability of healthy container plants. Planting and marketing of trees and shrubs may continue year-round in some southern regions.

Nurseries may be strictly wholesale in their marketing approach or strictly retail or a combination of both. The most logical strategy for beginners is to aim their product toward the retail customer. In the early stages of a business, it is difficult to grow enough plants to realize a satisfactory income if they are sold at wholesale prices. The lowest mark up at which a retail nursery can expect to show a reasonable profit is double the wholesale price, and this is only if you offer plants cash and carry, with no guarantee or special services.

Since most customers will expect plants to be guaranteed through the present growing season and will need rudimentary instructions, I suggest a retail price of two and a half to three times the wholesale price. Any further services offered to individual customers must be tacked on to this basic mark up. If you offer any type of installation or landscape service, it should be treated as an entirely different proposition from selling plants. Each service job must be priced individually by the amount of materials and time it will require. All plants going to a landscape job must be priced at retail.

Some inexperienced nursery owners are overanxious to make a big sale when customers want to buy a lot of plants or have a substantial landscape job done. You cannot give discounts for the larger sale because almost every one of the big purchasers will take full advantage of your guarantee. A large portion of small customers will never bother to redeem a plant guarantee even if they have a perfectly legitimate claim. In my experience, people who purchase a large amount of nursery stock are more likely to give you future headaches than are anonymous crowds whose purchases remain under $50.

Anyone who enters the nursery plant business should be fully prepared to give plenty of information about culture and planting, and to cheerfully refund guarantees as they are presented, even if the customer's claim is somewhat questionable. A miserly or grudgingly honored guarantee is worse than none at all. Arguments about guarantees are the fastest way to lose customers (and every other potential customer who is bound to hear their sad story).

Part of the fun of visiting a real nursery rather than a discount store sales yard is the possibility of finding new and exciting varieties. Most people want to plant something a little different from the ordinary. They also want to talk to someone who *really knows* how to grow trees and shrubs. This is why you have a tremendous market advantage if only it is capitalized upon at every turn. Consumers will gladly pay a little extra for the information, convenience, and confidence which you supply. Carrying unusual items is a service for which you must charge extra.

If you lack a suitable location for retail sales, or don't care to deal with individual customers, starting a profitable wholesale nursery may prove to be your piece of cake. It is more difficult but certainly not impossible. You must find a satisfactory niche which the larger wholesale nurseries are not servicing adequately or which they do not care to service. This usually means producing trees and shrubs which are somewhat scarce in the general marketplace or which require a good deal of individual hand labor.

Landscapers are often a good market for the wholesaler to pursue. A landscaper usually works under project completion deadlines and will gladly pay near retail prices for some special plants which are unobtainable elsewhere.

Whatever marketing strategy you pursue, it is essential to establish a consistent approach early and gear all production work towards a profitable fulfillment of these goals. **Growing plants without an established plan for marketing them profitably is a sure route to failure.** A good deal of advance planning is essential to arrive at a realistic and attainable marketing program.

EXAMPLE OF NURSERY
EXPENSES AND PROFITS

Some simple economic features about the type of small retail nursery you are likely to begin will now be depicted. This representation is simplified a good deal so that the main points are clearly observable.

In order to view our economic model in perspective, you must keep the qualifying points listed in Table 6 firmly in mind as you study Tables 7 and 8. One important point which must be stressed is that any initial monetary outlay for facilities or equipment has not been projected because it is assumed you already have a small plot of ground available or one which you can rent. The same is true for the transportation needed to complete landscaping jobs projected in the model.

Any incidental equipment needed for start up is included as part of the miscellaneous expenses. In order to be successful with very little risk, you must be willing to start with the bare essentials and work your way up. A new truck and comfortable office might be nice later on, but at the start you must make due with existing resources.

The size of nursery projected in this example is not likely to provide a livable family income, but merely represents what might be possible during the first year. The operation would need to be expanded a multiple of 2 or 3 times to support an average family in moderate style.

The costs represented in Table 8 could be lowered significantly by using recycled pots and by shopping around for less expensive tree or shrub starters or by growing some yourself. Prices paid could sometimes be less than one-half of those quoted if you took advantage of special promotions offered by suppliers.

The capital requirements necessary to start growing and selling nursery stock are not large if you begin very simply. Some landscaping work has been included in the economic model presented in Tables 8 and 9 primarily because it allows you to generate cash flow without significant capital investment. If you perform some landscaping work, fewer trees and shrubs need to be grown to produce the same income. This increases the chance of selling them all at good prices. Marketing plants profitably is a big challenge in the early years, and you must be cautious not to produce more than can be sold. Inventory carry-over is a major problem at some nurseries because they constantly produce more plants than they have developed a market for. A high carry-over rate causes you to spend a good deal of time caring for the previous year's plant inventory rather than growing new crops.

Doing some landscaping the first year will help you decide whether growing plants or installing them in the landscape is more to your liking. It will also provide a good idea of which activity is more profitable in the local area.

Plants could be sold wholesale by offering them to local garden centers, landscapers, or chain stores. However, you must remember the selling price would at least be cut in half, and it is not always easy to break into the wholesale market quickly. Most of these businesses order stock at least 6 months in advance, and they like to deal with established growers who they feel can deliver the merchandise reliably.

A retail operation with, perhaps, some landscaping services offered is the only way to earn a significant income the first few years without investing a good deal of capital.

Table 6

Qualifying statements which apply to Tables 7 and 8 of the nursery economic model which follows.

A. Owner will devote 1000 hours per year (equals approximately one-half of a normal 40 hour work week) to nursery operation and landscape projects.

B. Cost of care and culture for nursery crops is based upon approximate climatic conditions prevailing in the Midwestern United States.

C. Owner is physically capable of doing moderately heavy nursery and landscape work.

D. State law allows nurseries to containerize plants up to 30 days before sale in approved containers.

E. At least 10000 square feet of reasonably level land can be rented for nursery operations from the owners or others.

F. Water supply is available to nursery.

G. Model assumes 1 complete crop of 1000 containerized 5 gallon trees and 1000 2 gallon containerized shrubs. With 3% dumpage rate, the crop would be reduced to 970 containers of each crop.

H. Containers and plant material prices are taken from catalogs of reputable suppliers. They represent neither the highest nor the lowest prices.

I. All plants to be potted and purchased in a dormant state from specialist wholesale growers.

J. Assume plants will be sold retail at the growing location or through use on landscape projects contracted by the nursery owner.

K. Retail price of $35 for 5 gallon containerized trees and $17 for 2 gallon containerized shrubs represents the actual price received by the author's retail department in 1999. Guarantee of 6 months given with each purchase. Chain store prices are usually cheaper while some independent nurseries may charge more.

L. All plants are sold during the growing season immediately following containerization.

Table 7

Expenses involved in operating a small outdoor tree and shrub container nursery during the growing season. Limited landscape services offered. See text about ways to save costs.

Variable costs per plant unit produced

Container for 2 gallon shrubs $0.59
Soil for 2 gallon shrubs 0.40
Container for 5 gallon trees 0.86
Soil for 5 gallon trees 0.85
Dormant bareroot shrub for 2 gallon 3.00
Dormant bareroot tree for 5 gallon 7.25
Total variable cost per 2 gallon shrub $3.99
Total variable cost per 5 gallon tree $8.96

Fixed operational costs per year for nursery

Land rental for 10,000 square feet, 6 months $700
Fertilizer 250
Water 500
Pest and weed control 300
Liability insurance 500
Frost protection insulation fabric...200
Vehicle usage for 3000 miles at $0.30 per mile 900
Miscellaneous tools 300
Miscellaneous expenses 700
Total fixed operating costs $4,350

Table 8

Revenues, costs, and profits for operating a small outdoor nursery and landscape service during the growing season only. Refer to table 6 for qualifying statements.

Calculation of yearly revenues

Nursery produces 1000 2 gallon shrubs per year at
    a retail selling price of $17 each (1000 x $17) $17,000
Nursery produces 1000 5 gallon trees per year at a
    retail selling price of $35 each (1000 x $35) 35,000
Landscape contract work: 300 hours $30 per hour
    (300 x $30) 9,000
Total gross revenues per year **$61,000**

Calculation of yearly selling and production costs

Cost of advertising to promote business, assume 5%
    of gross revenues (0.05 x $61,000) $3,050
Extra landscape and sales help during busiest
    8 weeks of season at $7 per hour 2,240
Deduct 3% crop spoilage (0.03 x $52,000) 1,560
Fixed operating costs from Table 7..4,350
Variable cost of planting 1000 2 gallon shrubs
    (1000 x $3.99) 3,990
Variable cost of planting 1000 5 gallon trees
    (1000 x $8.96) 8,960
Guarantees redeemed for dead trees and shrubs at 5%
    of net plant sales (0.05 x $50440) 2,522
Total costs per year for selling and production **$26,672**

Calculation of before tax profits

Total revenues less selling and production costs
    ($61,000 – $26,672) **$34,328**

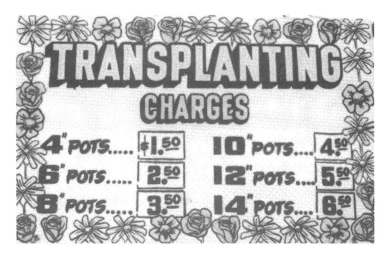

A transplanting service not only helps customers avoid a messy chore, but adds income to the nursery and assures the job is done properly. Charges in the photograph do not include the price of new pots.

Potting soil formulated and mixed at the nursery or greenhouse can be a big money maker. One of the highest profit items if it is properly presented.

The $34,328 projected earnings in Tables 7 and 8 for halftime work could be decreased greatly if you sold plants for only half as much at wholesale prices. There is opportunity in wholesale nursery production, but it takes money and time to become established.

The income realized from growing nursery stock can be greatly increased by also selling other related items. Seeds, fertilizers, garden implements, and plant care products are a few of the accessories which might be offered along with trees and shrubs. Your high quality plants will serve as a drawing card to attract customers for other services and merchandise.

There is a favorable long-term trend for tree and shrub sales. You need only to observe the major publicity trees have received on Earth Day in the last few years to realize that the general public is becoming more aware of the ecological significance plants have for the world environment. While many industries spend billions of dollars to promote their product, the nursery trade is receiving billions worth of free advertising!

THE MODERN NURSERY

The technological side of nursery production has not been emphasized in the previous discussion because most beginners in the industry will have neither the money nor technical background to employ the latest methods until they have had a year or two of experience. The technical aspects of production are of greater importance as one becomes more and more oriented toward wholesale production.

Modern nursery production methods, especially in the early stages of plant growth, may closely parallel the techniques used for greenhouse ornamental plant production. More and more culture of young nursery stock is taking place in the greenhouse as growers find that the extra cost of indoor facilities is more than made up by closer control which can be exercised over the crop. In fact, a modern nursery grower may find that training in greenhouse operation and culture methods is more important to the success of a nursery than is a good background in methods used outdoors. Of course, each production phase in a plant's life is important, but the trend is clearly toward more intensive culture during the juvenile stage.

The modern nursery, as it becomes larger, is also heavily dependent upon the proper use of machinery and pest and weed control methods. A large nursery can become almost impossible to run unless many of the essential tasks are mechanized. It is no longer possible to find laborers who will work in fields all day even if they are paid a handsome wage. This is another reason why many growers are moving a good deal of their plant production indoors.

Fortunately, by purchasing young plants from specialists, it is possible for an individual to get started in business without all the newest cultural facilities and machinery. Besides, it will take a few years to learn what types of modern techniques and facilities can be beneficially added into your operation as it grows. A lot of money should not be spent on this type of nursery improvement until it can be done wisely.

There are large scale wholesale nurseries in almost every state, and there are tremendous production areas in several regions which possess climatic benefits. Oregon, California, Tennessee, and Ohio all have large nursery concentrations. By visiting these areas, your vacation can be used to practical benefit, and many of the costs can be deducted as a business expense when tax time comes.

Personal Note from the Author:

Few experiences in life can be so gratifying as planting a nursery plot or large landscape with dormant bareroot stock and then marveling as the apparently lifeless trees and shrubs leaf out a few weeks later. However, when this miracle of life fails to materialize as expected, the agonizing sense of loss is equally felt.

This is why you must take care to offer healthy nursery stock which has every chance of fulfilling your customer's dreams. They will love you like a brother or sister if their dreams come true. Conversely, they will revile you as a charlatan if plants shrivel and wilt.

As customers judge you, so shall you judge your suppliers. A poor supplier can ruin your dreams and business by providing nursery stock which has been improperly treated. Investigate the integrity of every supplier carefully, especially those who provide dormant stock. A nurseryman's word must be his bond.

If your nursery provides only high quality plants that thrive as expected, word of mouth advertising will bring more business in the years ahead than can easily be handled.

Chapter 6

PRODUCTION AND MARKETING OF ORNAMENTAL PERENNIAL PLANTS

Perennial plants will be discussed separately from the greenhouse and nursery topics in this book because perennials are becoming more important as a horticultural crop and because their production and marketing is sufficiently different to warrant some special comments. Many businesses which we call nurseries are, in fact, specialist producers of perennial plants. Some greenhouse owners are now concentrating their efforts upon perennials.

There is no question that ornamental perennials are now receiving more public attention than in the past. Although perennials may have been proportionally even more important in the landscape before the current boom in annual flower usage arrived, they were primarily a private preoccupation. Gardeners would locate particular varieties they wanted and then trade seed and plant divisions amongst themselves. Perhaps the reason perennials are now becoming more commercialized is that a fast-paced lifestyle does not lend itself to leisurely treasure hunts and subsequent bargaining sessions for the required varieties. Many new gardeners have the impression that if they plant perennials, they will save time in the future since the plants will come back year after year and require very little care.

PERENNIAL BUSINESS EASY AND ECONOMICAL TO START

If you are looking for a horticultural business which you can start with very little money and operate part-time in your own back yard, this is it! A very high return on the time and money you invest is possible. Although there are several large growers on the national scene, and although perennials are often featured as mail order offers, there is generally a shortage of locally grown fresh perennials in almost every section of the country.

Of course, the amount of time and money you invest in a perennial plant venture will be the determining factor in how large and prosperous your business ultimately becomes, but it is easy to start in this specialty on a very small scale and gradually expand as your resources and interest grow. Other horticultural enterprises also offer this opportunity but perhaps not to the same degree.

Although the local gardening market for perennials is not likely to be as large as for annual flowers or nursery stock, it is generally less competitive. If the proper production and marketing methods are employed, it is possible to realize a greater percentage return for perennials than it is for the more common items carried in garden centers, plant stores, and mass outlets. For a small perennial grower, even the wholesale market may be a suitable entry point because a relatively high unit price is possible, and there are often no other local wholesale growers.

Because the total market for perennials is fairly small, most larger greenhouses and nurseries are reluctant

Perennials command premium prices in most localities. Even on sale, there is plenty of room for profit on these medium-sized plants.

to begin specific cultural and distribution programs involving them. The big operators want to move mountains of merchandise through standardized production schemes. They are not interested in limited-demand items. This is the perfect situation for small growers to supply the local market at highly profitable prices.

The costs involved in establishing a perennial plant business will vary greatly with the specific methods employed, but it is possible to get started with almost no initial outlay and very little operating expenses. This is truly a business which you can begin in your own backyard.

DIFFERENT METHODS OF PERENNIAL CULTURE

Perennials have undergone much the same change in culture from bareroot to containerization as have trees and shrubs, a small but growing proportion are also now being sold as juvenile seedlings straight from the greenhouse. The main reason why perennials have not developed into a large segment of the horticultural industry as yet is because growers have been unable to develop an economical method of containerization which allows reasonably priced plants to be sold in flower over a long period of time.

Containerization at an economical price can surely be achieved easily, I have done it myself. However, except for isolated varieties, it is not certain that perennials will be routinely brought into flower in these inexpensive containers. Much depends on what one considers inexpensive. My definition is that the price of flowering perennials should be fairly close to that of a bedding plant pack of flowering petunias or impatiens.

A good deal of university research is now being conducted to determine the correct cultural conditions necessary for flowering perennials in containers at will. This research is touching only a few out of thousands of varieties. It will be a long time before a wide spectrum of material can be flowered economically.

Why must perennials be in flower if a truly large volume of plants are to be sold? Because the average consumer will not as yet purchase nonflowering garden plants in any great numbers. This is just a fact of life! People buy flowers because they are pretty, and if a person cannot see the beauty at the time of purchase, it is left to the poor substitutes of pictures and imagination to convey the message. A lavish perennial display garden at the selling site is an easy way to double or triple perennial sales instantaneously. If people can see mature blooming plants in the landscape, it provides powerful incentive to buy.

A "flat" of excellent Coreopsis seedlings with color picture tags ready for sale or for transplanting into larger containers. You may produce seedlings on site or purchase them from specialist growers.

You, however, need not speculate about the future market for ornamental perennials. The present market size and price structure are favorable enough to make good money now.

For those of you who may not be familiar with the life cycle of perennials, I will provide a short outline and then show some of the ways perennials might be prepared for market. Perennials are reproduced by any number of means, depending upon the variety. Cuttings, root divisions, and seed propagation are the most common methods. Plants propagated in one growing season normally

**Color picture tags are essential if you sell perennials.
Not only do they give cultural information, they also
allow customers to know exactly what the flowers will
look like.**

need to be subjected to a cooler winter rest period before
they will bloom.

You can market plants in small containers as
actively growing juveniles shortly after propagation, in
which case they will not generally bloom in the garden
that season. Juvenile plants may also be stepped up to larger
containers or planted to the field, in either case being
subjected to cooler conditions through the winter so that
flowering occurs the following growth season. Perennials
which have been cold treated in the field can be sold as

dormant plants naked of soil or established in containers after digging. Plants which were containerized the previous year as juveniles are simply allowed to begin growth, or they may be stepped up again to larger containers before active growth starts in earnest.

Offering perennials in the juvenile stage with color picture tags results in quick turnover of inventory and a modest price to consumers. Dormant bareroot plants can be sold fairly inexpensively, but they allow only a very short time span for marketing. Planting cold treated bareroot plants or allowing cold treatment to take place after plants are established in larger containers results in perhaps the highest quality for consumer use but also the most expensive.

You will have to decide what the best method of handling perennials is for your particular situation. Bareroot marketing is declining in acceptability to most gardeners, so think very hard before choosing this alternative. All the details about cultural methods and marketing alternatives are contained in the book *Perennial Plants for Profit or Pleasure* listed in the back.

THE ECONOMICS OF GROWING AND SELLING PERENNIALS

A small plot of land which you own or rent can produce a tremendous amount of perennial plants if it is intensely managed. A square of your backyard measuring only 40 feet to a side can hold 3600 perennials potted in 1 gallon containers while allowing for aisle space.

If you sold these plants wholesale at $3 each, you would have an income of about $10,000 before a few

A group of one gallon perennials on sale in early season before significant bloom. This is the size of container specified in the accompanying tables.

modest expenses were deducted. Granted, this isn't enough income to make you feel rich, but it is very good money if you spend only a few hours a week working at it, and you have very little money invested. All you have to do is put in the same effort required by a large recreational garden plot. Table 9 outlines the economics of this type of enterprise if we assume rent is paid for a small piece of ground needed. The presentation is simple because the operation is simple.

Table 9

Expenses and profits of a small backyard perennial plant growing operation. Expenses can be lowered greatly by using recycled pots and starting plants from seed or cuttings rather than buying both items.

Purchase 3600 small plants from a propagator specialist
  at $0.30 each (3600 x $0.30) $1,080
Purchase 3600 gallon pots new at $0.20 each
  (3600 x $0.20) 720
Expenses of miscellaneous items:
  extra water, fertilizer, tools, pest control,
  insulation blankets for winter crops 600
Total expenses $2,400
Total revenues from selling 3420 one gallon perennials
  wholesale at $3 each. 180 plants or 5% of crop
  assumed wasted or lost. (3420 x $3) 10,260
Total profits ($10,260 - $2400) $7,860

Perennial plants are perhaps my first choice recommendation for those individuals who have a limited budget to begin a horticultural business. This type of enterprise can be started by almost anyone, anywhere. I favor marketing perennials primarily at wholesale for two main reasons. First, it simplifies the situation – you do not need to have a location suitable for retail activity, and you do not need to staff it all the time. Second, since perennials do not generally sell in big volumes, competition from larger growers is not usually severe. This situation allows you to make an adequate profit even when selling at wholesale. Most garden centers and mass outlets will welcome the opportunity to buy high quality local perennials because they have a hard time finding them.

NUMEROUS PERENNIAL VARIETIES
REQUIRE PROMOTION

As was mentioned previously, although it is growing rapidly, the perennial plant market is not exceptionally large at this moment. The gardening benefits provided by thousands of perennial varieties are not easily conveyed to the mass of consumers. A big pot of annual petunias in full bloom is its own best advertisement. Perennials are not generally of this gaudy, self-proclaiming nature; they bloom only briefly and then perhaps in a delicate manner. It takes an educational effort on the part of perennial growers and sellers to introduce the casual gardener to the many and varied benefits perennials can offer.

Although a well-planned display garden is the chief selling tool, color picture tags are a big help in marketing perennials. They let the consumer have some idea of what the plant looks like in bloom and can convey essential cultural information. Tags allow you to sell plants out of bloom and, thus, greatly extend the marketing season.

It is hard to imagine the extent of perennial plant diversity. There are literally thousands of varieties. This situation provides both advantage and disadvantage for the growers. Advantage in that it allows for continuous introduction of new cultivars to the market, but disadvantage in that consumers must be educated in the use and benefits of each introduction. The perennial grower must be willing to make this educational commitment in order to assure success. Much of your work in marketing perennials must be aimed at promoting products in an effective and economical manner. In perennials the old saying "the more you tell, the more you sell" is especially true.

Personal Note from the Author:

I personally prefer to grow plants such as geraniums and petunias (annuals) which virtually sell themselves when in bloom. Marketing perennials is a whole different ball game which requires a very active sales effort. This is perhaps why I have never sold the amount of perennials normally possible. It just isn't in my nature to leisurely attend to each individual customer.

If you are an avid gardener and like to talk to people, perennials may be right up your alley. Consumers desperately need and want information about the myriad varieties which are available.

Each person who engages in a horticultural business should make an effort to gravitate toward a specialty area which best suits their natural disposition. I have been most successful in the fast-paced business of colorful annuals — this risky and stressful specialty is not for everyone.

Chapter 7

THE RETAIL HORTICULTURAL BUSINESS

Most of you probably began reading this book because of an interest in growing plants for profit, not particularly in selling plants for profit. Plant enthusiasts, like myself, just naturally gravitate toward the growing end of horticulture. They don't generally get excited a great deal by the marketing aspects of business. However, if you want to make a living by growing plants, you must learn how to sell them profitably. There is no getting around this fact.

A few people actually like to sell plants more than they like to grow them, and some people are not in the proper situation to be growers. The following brief discussion is offered to those of you who find yourself in this category. I will deal with horticultural businesses whose primary activity is selling plants rather than growing them.

Although growing is my chief interest, I must admit that selling plants is usually the more profitable aspect of the horticultural business. Neither growing nor selling is more important, but, if we separate the two sides of the equation for close inspection, the act of selling is usually the more crucial factor which determines profitability.

This situation seems to be true in other commercial pursuits as well. The purpose in dwelling upon this fact is not to discourage you from a career in growing plants but rather to stress the importance marketing will have upon your business, and also to introduce the idea that perhaps your personal situation may be more amenable to a strictly retail horticultural business which requires no production or labor facilities.

RETAIL VS. WHOLESALE

A common mark up structure in retail shops is to price retail merchandise at double the wholesale cost. In plant and tree related businesses, the mark up may be 3 to 4 times wholesale if a good deal of service and a guarantee are offered. Floral shops may sometimes price flowers at 5 to 6 times cost when customers demand special treatment and unusually artistic arrangements.

This situation may seem lopsided in that tree growers could spend several years and flower growers several months in producing a crop, while their retail counterparts take as little as an hour or a month or two to sell the merchandise but reap as much or more of the total selling price.

Part of the disparity is explained, of course, by the fact that wholesale growers usually sell a larger volume per purchase, while retailers generally move only a few units to each customer. Furthermore, retailers also must perform other functions that growers do not, or perform to a lesser degree. Retailers must advertise or pay high rents to lure individual customers to their store, and they need to provide sales help to explain the product to consumers. The retailer must perform the hardest jobs in any business transaction: convince the customer that this product is (all things considered) the best deal of all and close the deal on the spot. If you have ever had much experience as a salesperson, you know how hard it is to accomplish these tasks.

Suffice it to say that most retailers truly earn their cut of the pie. There are certain persons who are instinctively better salespersons and deal makers than are the rest of us. These lucky few might be better off in the retail end of horticultural business rather than in the somewhat technical and time consuming production aspects. Retailing involves more of fulfilling dreams and desires of the customer more than does wholesale which focuses upon efficient management of conditions to produce a product.

The fact is that many horticultural businesses both produce plants and sell retail simultaneously. And many deal in two or more general plant groups at the same time in order to provide a sufficient volume of business.

A vertically-integrated horticultural business (one which both produces and sells the plant merchandise) is more often extremely successful than is one which is concentrated specifically upon growing or selling. However, there are some very sound reasons for beginning your horticultural career as a retailer only. For the sake of brevity, I will list these reasons in Table 10 and omit further comment unless it is essential.

Table 10

Primary reasons for beginning a horticultural business with special or sole emphasis upon retail aspects. Statements are generalized and will not be true in every case.

A. Retail requires less initial capital.

B. Allows you to learn about the business before committing capital and time to a growing operation.

C. You will develop a "feel" for the market possibilities before you implement costly growing programs to satisfy the market.

D. Smaller businesses can produce more sales volume per dollar invested by concentrating upon retail aspects.

E. The lead time required for entering a retail business is less than is necessary to begin growing crops.

F. With less money, effort, facilities, and inventory committed to a retail business, it is easier to abandon if it proves unsuccessful.

G. Allows you to place emphasis on one aspect of the business before engaging in another.

H. If your local market requires many diverse plant products, it may be easier to buy than to learn how to grow a diversity of crops.

I. Surplus of growers with a general lack of retailers in your area would make the retail business aspect look better relative to growing.

J. Retail allows you to concentrate time on offering a broad line of plant merchandise without having to learn the details of every variety.

K. While retailing requires a good deal of business knowledge, it does not require extensive technical knowledge about different varieties.

L. Retailing does not place a large inventory at risk to natural hazards when compared to a growing operation.

M. Growers are more likely to be subject to environmental regulation.

One of the drawbacks of retail business is that there is more competition in this arena. Many of the reasons for being a retailer or wholesaler are a double-edged sword. Seldom is a factor totally advantageous or deleterious. Business activity involves a process of choosing the most appropriate path to accomplish objectives. You must carefully weigh each alternative and select the one which will most certainly lead to success.

Each of the business opportunities discussed in this book could be entered from a strictly retail approach. Keep this in mind as you begin to evaluate the different options available.

Although I do not want to present a detailed discussion of how to run a retail business, I would like to mention one extremely important point. It concerns business location. If you have no production facilities or any other special attraction that will attract customers to visit your place of business, it is obvious that a retail store lives or dies primarily upon how well-situated the chosen retail location is in bringing merchandise and customers together. How much business you do will greatly depend upon the number of people who are exposed to your plants and related products. One of the primary ways of obtaining this exposure is by selecting a high traffic location. This means high traffic that is favorably disposed toward your product, not just high traffic in general. Everyone has heard the old real estate adage: "There are 3 key ingredients to success in retail business: location, location, location."

One means of obtaining such a location is to market cooperatively with high traffic grocery, hardware, discount stores, etc. Most of these entities have their own garden

Wide cement walkways provide convenient access for shoppers in this retail greenhouse. Knee level benches display plants at an ideal height.

and flower departments, but some of them are willing to lease space. This is often called "job racking" in the simplest form, but may sometimes allow you to enter into a formal lease arrangement for a period of years.

COMMON RETAIL BUSINESSES

The two most common independent retail horticultural businesses, by far, are flower shops and garden centers. Every reader probably has a general conception of these terms so that no further time needs to be wasted upon introducing them, but a few minutes discussing details may prove fruitful.

Flower and plant stores

Flower shops are common in every settled area — even smaller towns. They range from extremely upscale artistic boutiques down to simple "bucket" shops that sell plants and flowers almost as reasonably priced as those in supermarkets. The dollar volume of merchandise sold also varies from millions down to less than $100,000. I have personally mailed promotional material to approximately 45,000 individual shops in the United States.

This large number of shops tells you two things: 1) there is an opportunity in almost every locale; and 2) vast volumes of plants and flowers are sold each day. This means that wherever you live, there is a good chance that you could start a viable business in this line. Sure, there is already competition, but many of these shops are poorly managed and have numerous customers who would prefer to purchase their needs from a business that is more progressive and operated in a better fashion. The large number of shops already in operation only means that decorative flowers and plants is a massive business segment when the industry is considered as a whole. It does not mean that every business opportunity is taken up.

There is almost no end to the types of independent flower and plant stores. Some operate from a traditional store, others from a greenhouse, some as stalls in malls, hotels, hospitals, and airports; many are connected with pet stores, gift stores, garden centers, candy stores, etc. Some have no store except a toll-free telephone number over which orders are taken and then transmitted to local florists. This enumeration does not even consider the opportunities which may be open in mass market areas such as supermarkets, discount stores, and the like.

Garden centers

Although garden centers are often larger in terms of dollar volume than most flower stores, there is no hard and fast generalization that can be made in this regard. Almost every observation which was just offered for flower and plant stores can be made about garden centers. Only some details change – such as garden centers are often connected with a tree nursery, greenhouse, hardware store, farm implement or seed facility.

Several other types of retail businesses may come to your mind as we discuss additional horticultural specialty areas in the following chapter. Several of the ones mentioned could likely be focused primarily upon the retail phase.

Personal Note from the Author:

Although I am not primarily interested in the retail aspects of horticulture, it has been a necessary part of my business survival strategy.

One portion of retailing that I do like is when I can personally visit other production facilities to purchase plants, trees, or flowers to sell in my store. I love to "cherry pick" these growers and select only the very best merchandise which is (in my estimation)much more valuable than the listed price. This is just like taking candy from a baby. Of course, bargains can't be found at every stop, but, if you are prepared to purchase in volume, growers will almost always lower the price rather than lose a sale.

I have often thought this would be a most enjoyable way to pass time in retirement — traveling from one area to another making good deals and leaving the retail sales to someone who specifically handled that end of the business.

Of course, you must remember that bargain prices are no good unless you truly need the merchandise.

Chapter 8

ADDITIONAL HORTICULTURAL SPECIALTY BUSINESSES

There are many ways to make money by growing or selling plants or providing plant services. I have covered a few of the more likely and widely available opportunities in some detail. Perhaps you have not found a specialty among these which strikes your fancy, or none of them seems possible under the personal circumstance in which you find yourself. A brief listing of additional horticultural enterprises might help you find a more suitable choice to match up with your talents and resources.

These miscellaneous horticultural businesses will not be discussed at length for a variety of purposes. Mostly because it is a practical necessity to limit discussion of certain topics in order that the overall purpose of this book is not lost by excessive detail. However, you should not interpret my decision to abbreviate as an indication that any of these businesses are less worthy than the ones which have been treated more completely. Any one of the possibilities could be exactly what you are looking for and each could be highly profitable under certain circumstances.

The secret to financial success in horticultural specialty businesses will not be found in some universally applicable rule or equation but rather in finding the particular economic opportunity which allows you to take advantage of market forces special to the local surroundings. If these unique market forces can be matched with your natural talents, the combination can result in an amazingly successful business. There is no effortless way to find this happy combination; it takes a good deal of investigation regarding every available opportunity and some realistic soul searching to determine just what your special talents are. Hopefully, I will be able to start you in this process by pointing out some of the benefits and drawbacks to be found in particular situations.

In general, the following business opportunities are of a rather specialized nature, and their applicability may be limited to a narrow range of circumstances. The people who are active in these specialized fields sometimes lean toward an exaggerated view of how important and potentially rewarding their specialty is. They cannot be faulted greatly for this since it is likely we all engage in some of the same behavior in regards to our own areas of interest. But we must be aware of the situation and try to be as realistic as possible.

My caution to you is that as you read information about a specific field of interest or discuss it with promoters or activists, make sure all the facts presented seem to add up properly and that the overall proposition appears to make sense. While it cannot be denied that there are many legitimate business opportunities in every one of these fields, it is also true that a certain amount of self-serving exaggeration may sometimes overshadow the hardheaded economic facts when enthusiasts present their case to you.

In most of these horticultural specialty businesses, particularly if you start small, there is no need for high priced consultants, nor should you pay more than absolutely necessary for essential equipment. Carefully investigate any offers you receive to make sure they are legitimate and cost effective. I have seen more than one enterprise in horticulture where the only person to make money is the expert consultant or the individual who sells supposedly required equipment.

GREENHOUSE VEGETABLE PRODUCTION

Perhaps no other area of horticulture strikes the imagination as strongly as does growing vegetables, especially tomatoes, indoors. And with good reason: there is an almost unlimited demand for this crop. If vegetables could be produced in greenhouses at prices which were truly competitive with the open air farmer's price, we would witness the largest construction boom in greenhouses which has ever occurred.

Greenhouse grown vegetables can be sold only because they are of higher quality than field grown produce or because they are available when field crops are out of season. Crops grown indoors can seldom compete price-wise with those grown outdoors. This is the central fact why there is not more indoor production of food crops. When food crops are grown under cover, the very competitive and commodity-like nature of vegetable prices tends to make profitable operation of these greenhouses difficult unless efficient production methods are utilized.

Personally, I always purchase local vine-ripened greenhouse tomatoes because they taste so much better and because they are juicier. The price doesn't affect my selection because cheaper field grown tomatoes seldom have good flavor or substance — at least this is the case in my locale.

Throughout this book, I have stressed that the lucrative nature of the horticultural specialty crop is enhanced by their non-commodity-like market position. In other words, these specialty crops are relatively small so that institutionalized markets do not exist for them. Prices are struck between the individual producers and buyers, not established by an impersonal market force. This is the type of situation that favors smaller, innovative growers. Of course, everyone must realize that these markets we speak of differ only in degree. Individual farmers in the giant wheat market may occasionally be able to realize some competitive price advantage due to their shrewdness, and a greenhouse grower of petunias is often constrained somewhat by price structure prevailing in the informal petunia market. But, generally, the larger the market size, the more competitive pricing and production becomes.

Anyone who wants to begin a commercial greenhouse vegetable growing operation must evaluate the advantages and drawbacks of this business carefully. Demand for the product is immense, but prices are normally fairly low. Production costs can easily outrun the wholesale prices received for crops unless they are grown efficiently. There is not much chance of selling any significant part of your crops at near retail prices unless you develop specialized customers such as upscale restaurants and exclusive produce boutiques. The major established retail market channel for vegetables is, of course, in the supermarket.

Most successful vegetable greenhouses are fairly large, and they are generally located in population centers where quality produce of one variety or another is in short supply at different times of the year. The newer facilities being constructed today are usually highly automated and capital intensive. Some very large corporations have become active in this horticultural specialty, not always successfully.

Depending upon the tax codes applying at the time, there may be financial incentives other than simple buy and sell factors to consider when setting up a vegetable greenhouse. Some of these operations have shown tax shelter opportunities in the past. In certain locations, there is a tendency for local government agencies and economic development groups to help finance businesses which involve greenhouse vegetable growing. You may be lucky enough to find very favorable financing and business incentives offered in your area.

Ordinary people usually envision a vegetable greenhouse as one in which tomatoes are grown hydroponically (in nutrient solution without soil). In fact, leaf lettuce and cucumbers are probably the leading crops at present. There are many greenhouses which use some form of soil-like mixture as a growth medium rather than growing in gravel or water troughs. The nutrient supply may be basically similar to that used in pure hydroponics systems, but several methods for delivering this solution to the roots are presently employed.

One big advantage to greenhouse vegetable growing is that many equipment and material suppliers offer more-or-less cook book instructional services. Since a grower is often engaged in the production of a single variety, these standardized methods may be quite effective. Be advised, however, that there are many alternative methods. Do not rely blindly upon advice from someone else instead of using your own good judgement. A few companies claim to offer effective marketing services for growers who do not wish to be bothered with this phase of the business. Some of these marketing services are undoubtedly legitimate and perform a worthwhile service, but you should investigate them very carefully in order to avoid placing the important marketing functions of your business in jeopardy.

Since growing greenhouse vegetables is a popular subject, there are several excellent technical books to help the newcomer along.

If you are interested in this field, you should first check out the economics of marketing and growing in your area very carefully and realistically. Do not be overenthusiastic simply because the project seems glamorous. Evaluate equipment and material suppliers extensively for reliability and price. References from established growers should be checked out carefully before you make any substantial investment commitments. My personal opinion of the opportunities in this horticultural specialty is that it is not one of the easier businesses to enter on a limited budget. If you become involved, it should be with the idea of eventually expanding to a large enough size to compete efficiently. The existence of a large market and standardized growing methods are potential benefits under some circumstances. The extensive training sessions some suppliers provide are also very helpful.

HERB PRODUCTION AND MARKETING

The separation of herb and vegetable production into different topics is purely arbitrary. Except for some differences in market structure, most of the comments made about greenhouse vegetables could be applied equally well to herbs.

Although herbs have been grown commercially since time immemorial, it has only been in the last few years that much thought has been given them in the United States as a separate entity apart from other agricultural crops. Fresh herbs from greenhouses have especially received attention recently. Whether or not this notoriety will become permanently established remains to be seen. Fresh herb production indoors is concentrated in the more cosmopolitan population centers where demand is being spearheaded by use in exclusive restaurants. Supermarkets are beginning to pick up on the trend towards fresh herb use and routinely offer some of the more common varieties in their produce section.

If the current preoccupation with gourmet dining among the population continues, both indoor and outdoor culture of specialized herbs will skyrocket.

In some ways the herb market resembles that for flowers and ornamental plants. It is still rather small (as it is for ornamentals) when compared to more basic agricultural crops, and there is a wide assortment of varieties which are meant to be used under particular circumstances in food preparation, semi-medicinal treatments, scents, and other assorted purposes. This market structure lends itself to generally higher prices and offers opportunity for smaller producers to find a specialized niche which is highly profitable. One characteristic which the herb market does not share with ornamentals at the present is the existence of widespread independent retail opportunity. While flower shops, nurseries, and garden centers flourish in almost every small town in America, shops specializing only in herbs have not yet been able to become successful on so general a basis. Only where their popularity is greater and where sufficient population is present are special retail herb shops able to prosper.

Thus, although the wholesale price paid for herbs may be rather attractive in most locations, selling your herb product at retail prices is not always a viable option except in those areas where circumstances combine to allow enough volume for establishment of independent retail shops. The market for herbs is increasing. It is likely that within a few years herbs will become a major and stable horticultural specialty crop.

If you choose to enter this field, it is suggested that you be aware that demand for herbs could decrease rapidly if their appeal in gourmet cooking and semi-medicinal purposes wanes to any extent. Ornamental foliage plants suffered a similar fate a few years ago; there was near insatiable demand during the late 70s and early 80s when leading decorators and magazines promoted the use of interior plants, but, as these opinion leaders moved onto other interests, foliage demand decreased rapidly from the boom levels (in 2000 foliage plant production has regained its previous prominence).

I believe that if a sustained bonanza in herb production and sales is to become reality, it will result from demand related to their increased use in mainstream medical applications. In this situation, the prices of raw product are of little concern to consumers because quality factors and steady, year-round availability become the dominant requirements. If such circumstances developed, we could see prices for high quality medicinal herbs reach gold rush levels. However, local growers need to help develop a demand for fresh herbs rather than dried material or extracts. The latter products are too easily shipped from overseas where prices are generally low. People who take herbs medicinally or even for food should be very concerned about product safety. A local grower can more easily assure safe growing conditions.

There is now much preliminary activity in medical circles regarding derivation of medicines from plants (there has always been a good deal). However, as yet, not much of this activity has resulted in widespread practical opportunities for plant growers to fill specific needs for crops. This situation is changing rapidly and offers the potential for exceptional profits for those who are ready to take advantage of future demands. One only need witness the rush to find Ginkgo bilboa leaves or Kava root after their medicinal values were popularized to realize the potential demand.

MAIL ORDER HORTICULTURE

The idea of selling plants through the mail probably doesn't occur to a great number of people. After all, why ship plants hundreds or even thousands of miles to customers when you are surrounded by potential buyers in your neighborhood? There are a couple of good reasons: first, you may live in a rural location where customers are far and few between; second, you may wish to specialize in growing a particular variety or group of varieties for which there is insufficient local demand but which has significant potential on the national scene.

Selling by mail order can be one of the most profitable and worry free methods of doing business if

Table 11

Basic requirements which must be met to successfully sell horticultural products through mail order.

A. Product must possess weight, shape, size, and durability characteristics which allow for economical and safe shipping.

B. Plant products must be of such a nature as to reach the customer in good shape even when subjected to the normal rigors of shipping processes (heat, cold, rough handling).

C. Sufficient product line must be available to generate a critical mass of total sales. Alternatively, a single product must be popular enough to generate profitable income.

D. A customer list must be developed for use in selling additional products.

E. Products must conform to requirements of shipping companies and to national, state, and local laws.

F. Product must possess characteristics which allow it to be advertised effectively and economically.

G. Product must actually satisfy customer so future orders will be made by that customer.

H. The mail order offer package must be designed to yield a profitable combination. Components of the offer are product, price, advertisability, audience, volume, and all the various aspects which integrate with one another to form the total offer.

I. An advertisement must be constructed which presents the offer in terms that pull enough orders to be profitable.

J. All sales must be carefully recorded and evaluated to determine the effectiveness of different aspects of the total mail order offer. Examples: orders resulting from advertisements in different magazines must be tabulated to determine which magazines were profitable and which were not.

certain basic requirements are satisfied. Table 11 lists the most important points necessary for a successful mail order plant business. There is no need to limit your mail order effort to plants; non-plant horticultural products are even easier to handle and ship by this means.

The biggest mistake prospective mail order entrepreneurs usually make is to expect that a single hot merchandise item will make their business successful. Mail order is like any other business: profits are normally built up over a period of time as a customer base is accumulated. New products are then added and sold to existing customers.

Mail order can be a rewarding method of making money, but success does not magically appear. A person seldom becomes rich in mail order by getting a flash idea, running a few advertisements, and then simply waiting for cash to arrive in the mailbox. The thousands of mail order super-schemes you see advertised are nothing but scams. Only one in a million get rich without hard work and perseverance.

Don't give up if you fail to make money on the first try. Sometimes it takes several experimental attempts before the right elements of a mail order offer are brought together in a profitable combination. But when this is accomplished, it can mean a lasting source of relatively trouble-free income. It has taken me over 10 years to develop a profitable mail order business in horticultural books, but, now that all the details have been worked out, I get orders everyday from all over the world. This adds a significant second income which now requires little effort.

People like to purchase by mail order if they can feel safe about sending their money to you. An ironclad guarantee of satisfaction is the best way to convince customers to part with their money. If your offer is legitimate, an unconditional guarantee will result in a very low percentage of returns.

Mail order is convenient for everyone concerned. You do not have to leave your place of business, and the consumer receives their merchandise at their front door. What could be easier? This is why companies often receive a higher price for merchandise through mail order than if it was sold in a conventional store. Mail order saves customers time and travel expenses.

INTERIOR AND EXTERIOR LANDSCAPING

Many individual firms providing interior and exterior landscaping services do not actually grow any significant proportion of the plant material which is used in their work. Being both a grower and a landscaper allows you to develop an increased expertise about plants and provides access to a ready inventory of plant material for installation jobs. However, operating in two specialties requires more time and capital.

In its simplest aspects, a landscaping business may be started with almost no capital or previous experience. This is why there are so many small operators to provide competition in this field. In order to stand out from the crowd, you must develop an expertise which customers will immediately recognize. If you don't, they will do the job themselves or hire the neighborhood handyman.

When deciding how much you should charge for your services, it is essential that careful account be taken of exactly what you have to offer. Your fee should include a basic charge for the actual work to be done and a premium

Local businesses and government entities are important sources of landscaping income. Many jobs do not require project design; they entail only proper installation of vegetation.

on top of this for the knowledge and expertise you contribute.

True landscaping is a combination of technical and artistic work. Hopefully, you can offer both services in the ideal mix. If you aren't an artist, don't worry, most jobs require only that you be able to organize and carry out a technically correct plant installation project. As was mentioned previously, there are computer programs, books and programs from professional landscaping organizations in most states that can help a lot. *The Illustrated Handbook of Landscape Plants* listed at the back of this book is a good place to locate preliminary information about jobs. It can also be used as a marketing tool to show customers what plants will look like.

Landscaping pays the best when you specialize in commercial or public projects and buildings. Small jobs for the individual homeowner are less complicated but generally offer less opportunity for profit. However, the big commercial jobs usually go to firms with an established track record of financial and technical capability. You will have to work your way up to the plum jobs. Most commercial and public landscape projects are awarded on a bid basis, which means you must be in position to receive notification when a job is coming up for bid.

Well-known firms receive bid notifications from architects, parks directors, or general contractors. New entries to the landscape business will have to seek out opportunities to bid on jobs. Most localities have a bid newsletter or notification service to which landscapers can subscribe. This service allows you to quickly pinpoint potential landscape jobs without running all over town to different job sites; it also allows you to get your bid in early before contracts have already been awarded.

Submitting a bid for landscaping services is no easy job. It is often the critical ingredient to success. An inflated bid proposal might lose you the job while too low a bid will result in a financial loss on the project. Costs must be estimated realistically for all aspects of the job which you are expected to complete. Do not leave any detail up to question.

Unexpected difficulties on the job site are one of the most common reasons why contractors lose money on landscaping projects. Look the job over carefully and try to foresee problems which might arise. When your cost estimate is complete, add about 5% to compensate for unpredictable difficulties. Sometimes no unforeseen problems will be encountered, but, in other cases, their cost will exceed 5% of the job total. Bidding manuals are available which will help you estimate costs for complete jobs.

You will not get far in the landscaping business unless a realistic guarantee is offered and honored. In the long run, it is better to ask a few dollars more for services in order to provide liberal guarantees which do not place an undue burden of proof upon the customer.

Most readers of this book are aware that outdoor landscaping is a common service in almost every town. Many of you might be surprised at the opportunities available in landscaping building interiors. This is a fast growing industry and offers a good deal of opportunity, especially to those people who find outdoor jobs too physically demanding. Indoor jobs generally do not require as much heavy work, and you are not subjected to extreme climatic conditions. Many of the specifics for indoor landscaping will parallel information mentioned above for outdoor services.

As public buildings, malls, offices, and other structures are constructed larger and fancier, indoor landscaping becomes more popular. Big jobs can easily cost more than $100,000. In addition, these jobs can often turn into a permanent contract for plant care.

PLANT CARE SERVICES

Given the busy lifestyle of today's families, the plant care field can only grow in volume and variety of work available for the horticultural specialist. The problem with this field, as with landscaping, is that everyone who needs a few extra dollars believes they can turn a profit caring for other people's plants.

In order to avoid the often unprofitable and unrewarding competition with amateurs, you must carefully and deliberately distinguish yourself from the crowd by stressing the knowledgeable, professional, and completely reliable nature of your services. There are many businesses and individuals who will gladly pay extra for the peace of mind your expert plant care brings when compared to that provided by on-again-off-again amateurs.

Everyone is familiar with the variety of plant care services offered to private consumers for their lawns, trees, and gardens. What you may not realize is the tremendous demand for these and further services which originate in the business and public sector. Most businesses would prefer to have a reliable expert taking care of their indoor and outdoor landscaping rather than taking one of their own workers away from his or her normal duties. There are often formal union or informal professional rules which prevent employees from working outside their expertise area. Do you think the Postal Service or the Internal Revenue Service dares ask regular employees to fertilize the lawn or shine leaves on indoor plants?

Although there is currently a good deal more potential work for plant care specialists in the outdoor landscape, the need for care of indoor plants is growing rapidly and there is probably less competition in this aspect. Working with indoor plants has several advantages: it is cleaner and less physically demanding; it is less seasonal in nature; and it generally requires less equipment.

Whether you care for plants indoors or out, there are a couple of points you must remember to be successful. First, repeat customers will eventually be the backbone of your business; you must be reliable, courteous, and do a good job in order to expect their future business. These valuable characteristics should entitle you to adequate compensation. Ask for reasonable payment in return for the knowledge and diligence you provide. Second, don't take on jobs which are so small as to make it impossible to turn a profit. Travel time and entering the job site can take up a lot of the day if you accept assignments which offer only a few minutes of actual work. You must charge the customer not only for the time spent on the job, but also for the time it takes to schedule the appointment, travel to the job site, present a bill, and take care of bookwork afterward.

You can get into the plant care field, either indoors or outdoors, with very little capital, and there is lots of work available if you look for it. On the other hand, you face a battle convincing customers that your expert services are worth more than the many amateurs willing to work cheaper. A sales program emphasizing the many benefits of expert care must be developed. Simply walking in and asking for the job will not generate much work, especially if your prices are higher.

TURF AND TREE CARE

These two categories of plant care are mentioned separately because they comprise a very large and potentially profitable portion of horticultural services. We have just mentioned some of the important aspects such as reliability and professional image, but it is also necessary to understand that turf and tree care are rather technical fields if they are done properly. There are a host of subjects the supplier must be proficient in so that customers receive a valuable service rather than haphazard or even damaging amateur work.

Turf and tree caregivers must at least understand the basics of plant growth, varietal differences, soil and water management, fertilizer applications, pest, disease, and weed control, and plant response to various treatments. Unless you provide services which are based upon a good degree of factual knowledge in these subjects, you cannot expect to be paid much more than the neighborhood handyman.

In addition to technical proficiency, turf and caregivers must organize their business in a manner which assures an efficient use of time, employees, and equipment. To sum it up, you should think of your venture as a *real* business rather than simply an unorganized sideline which competes with unemployed teenagers and other people who are simply mowing lawns for pocket change.

This point is amply demonstrated by the untold permanent damage created through inexperienced people cutting the tops off trees and calling it a pruning job, or by the death of surrounding shrubs and trees after a know-nothing lawn person has sprayed weed killer indiscriminately. I see cases like these and other serious problems almost weekly in my work. You should stress this point as you negotiate with potential customers who think it is less expensive to hire a nonprofessional.

In many localities arborists must be certified by the city government or through the state. A few areas may require certain aspects of turf care to be licensed. Every commercial applicator of insecticides, pesticides, and herbicides must be licensed and provide documentation of each application they make. These requirements should not present any obstacle to your entering the plant care field since the tests and programs leading to certification are generally free or very inexpensive and easy to pass. In fact, the licensees, when obtained, provide you with proof of expertise. Homeowners and business people will be unlikely to hire anyone who lacks these credentials once you point out to them that the **law** requires such certification.

Another factor which customers should be aware of is the fact that you carry liability and property damage insurance (you certainly should!).

HORTICULTURAL THERAPY SERVICES

Why are gardening and related horticultural pastimes the most popular leisure activities in the United States? Is it because they offer us a chance to save money on food products or the opportunity to make money increasing the value of a home? While some enthusiasts do achieve these practical goals, the great majority indulge in this hobby because it gives satisfaction, a bit of physical exercise, and, above all, a chance to relax and forget the mental pressures which life brings.

Mental health experts and physical therapists have long realized the benefit which horticultural activities offer the human mind and body.

Horticultural therapy programs are common at many institutions, but it is almost impossible to locate such service programs which are available to individuals once they are no longer associated with an institution on a regular basis.

Providing well-conceived horticultural programs and products for people to use in continuing, non-institutional therapy is one of the most neglected areas of horticultural business. It is a field which offers the possibility of extremely attractive financial awards while simultaneously reducing the suffering of human beings. Since this field is not truly established, not much can be said about how to proceed in setting up a business which specializes in it.

One thing which is obvious is that the people who enter this type of business should have a background in mental or physical therapy, as well as horticulture. Integration of these two elements composing a therapy program is a necessity.

Any therapy program must be well-coordinated with established health and mental care institutions and professionals. No one could hope to be successful in this type of service unless the program evidenced unquestioned professional expertise and enjoyed a positive relationship with potential referring institutions and professional individuals.

Under existing concepts of insurance coverage and public aid programs, it is likely that horticultural therapy services would have to be financed by the individual person receiving benefits unless the therapy service was associated with or prescribed through agencies or individuals recognized by the insurance companies or public aid programs.

As with any new and relatively untested concept, there would be many problems associated with developing a horticultural therapy service. *The reward for pioneering into territory where the fee structure is already high and competition is nonexistent could be immense.* This field of service is in approximately the same stage of development that home health care was 10 or 20 years ago. Home health care is now one of the fastest growing business segments in America.

MISCELLANEOUS HORTICULTURAL SERVICES AND PRODUCTS

We could continue indefinitely listing and discussing horticultural specialties which can be engaged in for profit. The projects presented in this chapter appear to be the most likely candidates for business opportunities in which large numbers of horticultural enthusiasts could participate easily. They are suitable, with few exceptions, to almost every locality in the United States, Canada, and Mexico.

If none of the specialties mentioned appeals to you as a business proposition, or, if each one offers little likelihood of success under your particular circumstances, don't despair! With a little research and imagination, you can create an original idea for commercial application which is uniquely suited to your special interests and resources.

Perhaps you live on a farm in a completely rural area and feel there is little you can do to participate in the horticultural success story. Have you ever thought about raising wildflower seed, or Christmas trees, or lawn sod, or perhaps dried herbs and flowers on at least part of your acreage? Each of these horticultural specialties can be done fairly profitably if you have the wherewithal and farming expertise to participate effectively! Most of my readers do not have access to the amount of land, water and machinery necessary for these operations, but perhaps they are already part of your present farm operation.

Some localities may possess special advantages which have not been recognized for certain horticultural crops. The advantage may be one of proximity to new markets, climate, or other factors. Perhaps your area has abundantly available substrate for mushroom culture or maybe it possesses the climate and water resources which are perfect for growing aquarium plants. Who knows?

The only way you can identify these more unusual opportunities is to make yourself aware of all the exotic horticultural activities people participate in and then see if any of these appear to fit in with your local conditions. A good way to locate possible opportunities is to go through advertisements, especially the classified, in horticulture-related magazines. Don't be discouraged because someone else already does a certain thing; this only means it is potentially profitable.

My own situation is a case in point. Although growing and selling ornamental plants has been very financially rewarding to me, I have almost exhausted the market potential in my sparsely populated region. Besides,

I am interested in areas of horticulture other than strictly growing and selling. After a good deal of thought and research, the idea popped-up that my educational and business background would provide the necessary ingredients for a successful sideline in horticultural writing. I can't say that I've gotten rich from writing, but it has provided a significant second income, and it is a rewarding endeavor in itself.

This is the type of personal exploration you need to perform in order to identify the opportunities best suited for your circumstances. I'm sure you will find some field of horticultural work that offers financial security while also enriching the other aspects of life. Refer back to Chapter 1 (Table 1) for a more complete listing of miscellaneous activities in horticulture.

Personal Note from the Author:

Success seldom comes on the first try — no matter what field you are working in. I can remember that in college I studied various chemistry and mathematic principles time after time before the light finally dawned and I was actually able to adequately understand the subject.

My business experience suggests that a similar process also operates in the practical world. Each personal success in the greenhouse and nursery business has followed a long period of knowledge gathering, trial and error, and fine tuning. My mail order venture required the same dogged persistence.

You may experience a good deal of initial success in a horticultural business, but you must also expect a fair share of failures. If you learn from every error, eventually a series of profitable products and services is built up, which combines with others to form a highly successful total business program.

The secret of wealth building lies not so much in creating one or two extremely profitable projects, but in accumulating a number of moderately successful product and service entities which comprise a larger overall business. This multifaceted business is safer to operate since hard times in one segment will often be balanced by average or better than average performance in another aspect.

Part III

HOW TO GET STARTED AND SUCCEED IN BUSINESS

People who enjoy learning how to grow plants usually have some favorable character traits which are useful in the business world. Horticulturists must be patient, willing to work hard, and acutely observant of their environment. Each of these attributes is critical to success in business. On the other hand, horticulturists are notoriously poor practitioners of the various administrative, marketing, financial and personal management activities which we normally expect are the special domain of the business person.

While you need not be a Wall Street genius to succeed at some form of horticultural business, at least the most elementary management activities must be attended to in order to avoid financial chaos. If you cannot force yourself to perform these essential business-related details, one option is to take on a partner who is willing and able to do so. Another option is to make use of a financial planning and accounting service.

Whether some of the strictly business-related activities of your enterprise are farmed out or done personally, only you can determine the more basic strategic concepts which will influence the general success or failure of the business. You are the one who will ultimately suffer if important business decisions and actions are left unattended. In addition to formulating a sound horticultural program, adequate plans for the business-related aspects of your entrepreneurial venture must be made. Remember, you are running a business, not indulging a hobby.

Part III of this book will give you an outline of how to start a successful business and how to make sure being in business accomplishes the ultimate goal of leading a happy and rewarding life. I will not attempt to provide details about particular subjects unless it seems that they are especially relevant to a discussion of a business in horticulture. If you wish to investigate certain business concepts further, most local libraries contain many books which pertain to a small business operation. Another fertile source for business information is the Internet, particularly the sites provided by the United States Small Business Administration and similar agencies in most states.

Chapter 9

COLLECT INFORMATION AND DEVELOP A PLAN

Now that you have surveyed the general field of specialty horticulture and learned a few details about particular business opportunities, perhaps you have decided to take the plunge and start an exciting new venture. The first task is to develop a concrete and effective course of action which will lead to success. In order to devise a plan, it is necessary to gather more detailed information about the chosen field of activity. Basically, you need to build a business plan which addresses the specifics relating to marketing, product production or supply sources, and general business practices.

This task could be approached like some major companies and institutions do: by hiring a consultant. More than likely, however, you do not have the kind of money these consultants want for their time. You can probably do an adequate job of research and planning if you work hard at it. Let's face it, the practice of hiring consultants arises in a large part from the desire of individuals to cover their backside. If something goes wrong with the project, they can always blame the consultant instead of themselves.

HOW TO FIND INFORMATION

Where can the type of information you are looking for be found? The most obvious and inexpensive source is in quality books. A couple of hours with a run-of-the-mill consultant will most likely cost $500. For this amount, you could buy 10 or 20 books about the subject and feel reasonably confident that the authors of these books are some of the most well-informed and successful members of the horticultural industry. As a source of the basic information needed to run a business in horticulture, there is simply no economical substitute for books.

Trade magazines are another informational bargain. Although magazines will not give the type of well-organized knowledge you can get out of books, they will include new cultural and variety developments, product news, advertisements from suppliers, and general industry news about trade fairs and seminars. A look at the Literature section in the back of this book will provide a good start in locating the most useful books and trade magazines for your business enterprise.

The Internet is fast becoming a critical source of free information on almost any topic, including horticulture. Internet presentations are often still in the development stage, so don't expect too much until the use of this vehicle becomes more common.

Some of the major means of gathering information have already been discussed in chapters 2 and 3 of this book. There is no need to emphasize the sources of information any further; however, it should be stressed again that after deciding to enter business in a particular field, you will need to gather as much factual information as possible. Concrete business plans require specific data rather than nebulous general impressions.

At this stage, as much numerical data as possible about the marketing and financial aspects of the planned new business needs to be accumulated. This process is not easy, and seldom can you expect it to yield answers with more than a 10% range of accuracy. But 10% to 20% accuracy is better than relying on wild guesses. Numerical data forces you to think in exact terms rather than simply daydreaming about generalities which could be totally erroneous.

Some of the information gathered from different sources may be confirmed by making private surveys concerning prices, amounts of plants sold by different outlets, and customer preferences. It is no trouble to gather price data; all you need to do is visit a number of establishments and write down the prices or obtain a price list.

As concerns volume, a rough estimate of sales made by different outlets can be tabulated by simply observing their operations for sample periods of time while recording each sale by the amount and type of merchandise involved.

Customer preferences may be harder to uncover since most customers observed will simply be reacting to the merchandise placed before them rather than selecting what they would really like if it were available. Some of this difficulty can be overcome by actually interviewing a number of potential customers to determine what their likes and dislikes are.

BASIC BUSINESS PRACTICES

There are some routine mechanics to observe no matter what type of business is being set up. You should become aware of all the local, state, and federal laws and regulations which apply to business in general. On the local level a list of general requirements can be obtained by visiting the city and county administrative offices. Be particularly careful to pick up a copy of local zoning regulations, and make sure you understand them before making any decisions about locating a business enterprise.

The office of the Secretary of State is usually a good place to begin when dealing with state government, then proceed to contact the Department of Revenue and Taxation and the Department of Labor.

The federal government will, of course, want you to report all income to the Internal Revenue Service and periodically provide information to the Social Security Administration and Department of Labor.

The U.S. Department of Commerce can often provide statistics which may be valuable to new businesses — for horticulture, one of their chief agencies (The Weather Bureau) has a wealth of local weather statistics available.

Horticultural businesses have some special regulations and agencies to deal with. The state department of agriculture usually issues permits for greenhouses and nursery production and sales. They will probably inspect your premises annually. It may be a good idea to check with the local health department to see if they have any regulations which might apply to the particular business started. Federal and state environmental agencies have numerous guidelines which must be followed concerning pesticide use and fertilizer runoff at your business site.

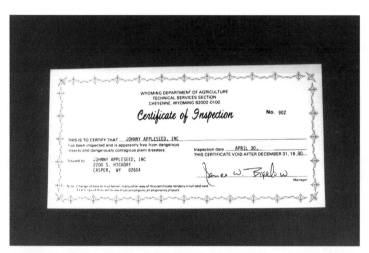

Most states periodically inspect each business engaged in production or sales of horticultural merchandise. Even in those states where strict compliance with regulation is enforced, such inspections seldom turn up significant violations if normal good housekeeping procedures are followed.

Although I have mentioned the more important regulatory agencies which interact with businesses, there may be some minor ones which are specific to your locality. The local Chamber of Commerce can provide information on this point. Not all these agencies will affect you equally. Zoning laws have great significance when a business first begins or if it relocates, but, after you are in compliance, they can be put on the back burner. Agricultural regulations in some states are only a formality, but in others, such as California, they must be observed carefully to avoid citation for violation.

All these laws and regulatory agencies may give you second thoughts about going into business. You have probably heard at least one horror story reciting the dire consequences which await any business person who steps out-of-line. Don't be a worrier, most of these regulations affect businesses only infrequently, and, if a little common sense is employed to understand the law and comply with it, life will go on with only occasional incidents. The situation is no different than making sure you obey traffic laws to avoid an unpleasant conflict with the police.

It may seem unusual to consider the Internal Revenue Service as a friend, but, if it were not for the requirements of complying with IRS regulations, many small businesses would totally neglect even the rudiments of financial record keeping. The necessity of monitoring financial activities would seem to be obvious to any business person, but I have seen many businesses fail because the owner had no idea about the financial health of the company. The situation in business seems to be no different than with the general public: there are those that know what their financial status is, and there are those that pay little attention to this aspect of their lives until financial calamity strikes.

Without a huge amount of luck, no business can survive over the long-run unless a system is set up to keep track of routine financial activities. Not only does such a system keep you appraised of the immediate economic status of the company, but it can help you make decisions which will affect future operations.

Not many business people enjoy this record keeping activity. Fortunately, there are accountants and bookkeepers who are happy to take it off your hands. Many small business owners find that it is more pleasant and more economical to have a professional accountant record and process all financial data. Even paychecks, social security payments, and taxes due are handled by accountants. A financial summary can be generated periodically to help you evaluate the financial status of your business. This is a great planning aid.

Of course, accountants do not work for free. These services cost money. Only you can decide if they are worth the extra expense. I strongly suggest that if you find yourself avoiding record keeping responsibilities, seek out a qualified accountant or bookkeeper to handle this chore. Be sure to shop around. Some accountants charge reasonable fees while others are high priced. You can talk to some in a relaxed manner while others charge you for every minute you are in their office.

Bookkeeping, business management, and tax programs for keeping track of your business on computer are numerous and very helpful if you are computer literate — if you aren't, it could be very advantageous to develop at least minimal skills in this respect.

FORMULATE A STEP-BY-STEP PLAN

The object of gathering information, learning laws and regulations, and exploring methods of monitoring your business is to develop a detailed step-by-step business plan. Devising a written business plan will help immensely by allowing you to focus your energy upon individual activities at the proper time. If the job of starting a business is carried out in an unorganized manner, much of your time and effort will be wasted. Breaking the job into smaller portions will help you accomplish objectives in human-sized bites. This process may even prove to be enjoyable as the problems seem to disappear, one-by-one, in orderly fashion.

Any business plan you formulate should have a timetable in which each specific task is given a definite starting and completion date. Of course, you will not always be able to stick rigidly to the timetable. Some jobs will take more time than planned while others will take less. Flexibility must be allowed in this case and for problems that turn up unexpectedly. Your business schedule is meant as a management aid, not as a beast which makes life miserable. Don't panic each time you can't stick to the plan religiously; these things happen.

LEARN FROM FIELD TRIPS

There is no better way to gain insights into the ornamental plant industry than to observe how it works on a daily basis. The practical experience gathered while actually visiting horticultural facilities can be used to reinforce and amplify written information. And, in many cases, you will pick up facts and general impressions in the field which were not fully expressible by the written word.

If you wish to work or operate a business in horticulture, carefully planned visits to all sorts of facilities will provide invaluable background information upon which to base future decisions. Field trips broaden your knowledge while working on daily problems.

Even serious amateurs who have no commercial interests can benefit from planned visits to horticultural facilities. The following field exercises direct attention toward some specific operational details which the average person is unlikely to notice with a casual visit.

The specific field trips listed below are arranged into groups which display common characteristics and which will require similar observational techniques. By arranging them in this manner, it is possible to reduce the number of individual forms required and thereby make it easier for participants to concentrate upon learning new material. Each general group of field exercises can be completed by using a common form for that group (participants are authorized to make photo copies of these forms for multiple use and should do so before any answers are filled in). This exception to copyright law is granted by Andmar Press only to the original purchaser of *Make Money Growing Plants, Trees, and Flowers* and only for the personal use of the buyer. **Do not write in this book if borrowed from the library.**

You will undoubtedly find that field trips to wholesale and retail facilities and to shows will be more beneficial for immediate business purposes. Don't overlook, however, the long term benefits which might come from visits to libraries, botanical gardens, etc.

LIST OF POSSIBLE FIELD EXERCISES

A. Plant production facilities
    1. Greenhouse
    2. Tree or shrub nursery
    3. Sod farm, lawn grass
    4. Christmas tree farm
    5. Herbaceous perennial farm
    6. Cut flower farm

B. Sales facilities
    1. Chain store indoor plant sales
    2. Chain store outdoor plant sales
    3. Independent flower shop
    4. Independent garden center
    5. Herb store
    6. Farmers market

7. Wholesale market, generally cut flowers

C. Landscape and conservation projects
1. Private homes, neighborhoods
2. Estate gardens
3. Business, theme parks, etc.
4. City, state, county parks; university, college, major building landscapes
5. Highway installations
6. Mines, dams, industrial reclamation
7. Interior plant displays in malls, convention centers, major buildings

D. Institutional facilities
1. University and college greenhouse gardens
2. Arboretums (tree collections)
3. Botanic gardens
4. Test gardens associated with seed companies, agricultural extension, private & public displays
5. Non-commercial greenhouses
6. Parks department plant growing operations
7. Government plant facilities—Forest Service, Dept. Agriculture, etc.
8. University experiment stations
9. Public gardens

E. Shows, meetings, organizations
1. Master Gardeners organization
2. Local garden club
3. Plant society meetings
4. Horticultural trade shows
5. Garden and horticultural tours

6. State or national horticultural meetings

7. Home and garden shows

F. Library facilities
1. Public library
2. University, college library
3. Agricultural extension library
4. Botanic garden, public garden, arboretum
   libraries

HOW TO PREPARE FOR AND CONDUCT FIELD EXERCISES

Field trips can be an invaluable source of information if they are performed conscientiously. They can be a total waste of time when preparation and careful execution are lacking. Be sure you plan ahead to make your trips successful.

Many of the suggested locations for field exercises will obviously be familiar to you. But there are others which you will need to locate in the phone book or through other sources. Local garden enthusiasts, the Agricultural Extension Agent, garden clubs, owners of horticultural businesses, parks directors, and college horticulture teachers are likely sources where you will also be able to find the locations of facilities for potential field trips.

Not every locality will have a full spectrum of horticulturally related facilities for you to visit. But at least 1/2 of the ones listed should be present in or near every small town.

Look over the prepared field exercise forms carefully before you arrive at a facility. Resolve any questions you might have about the forms before you begin work.

Be sure you know how to fill them out properly and that you have a general idea of what information you are looking for. If you are well prepared, you can spend the time available for productive work rather than organizing preliminary details which should have been taken care of previously.

There are some further points to consider when planning a field trip. Most of them are concerned with courtesy to the operators of the facility or with your personal comfort.

- Make sure you realize the difference between public facilities and those which are considered private. Libraries, botanic gardens, garden shows, retail sales areas, etc. are generally open to the public and require no advance notice to visit. Plant production facilities, reclamation sites, private estate gardens, seed company test gardens, etc. usually will require advance contact to make certain an educational visit is allowable. There are some sites which might fall between the two extremes (such as small independent retail shops, parks department facilities, university greenhouses, garden club meetings, etc.).
- If you are in doubt about whether you need permission — ask. It will seldom be denied if you are courteous and explain the purpose of your visit.
- Make sure the operators of private facilities know you are not a nosy inspector or potential competitor.
- If the trip involves outdoor work, dress properly for the weather. Be prepared for mud and cold or dry and hot weather. You may encounter both in the same day.
- Try to visit outdoor facilities during good weather.
- Watch your step—especially in production areas. Numerous hazards may be present.
- Use the rest room before you depart. Some places may have minimal or hard to locate facilities.
- Choose a good time of the year when there is plenty of interesting activity going on. Many horticultural facilities

have very seasonal activity patterns. But don't choose the very busiest days of the year—the owner or manager will often deny access at these times.

- Don't pester the employees or manager. A few questions may be permitted at private facilities but more are a nuisance. In public facilities, it is OK to ask lots of questions—the people are there to help you.
- You should visit facilities of different size and different emphasis. Don't simply choose the biggest and best. There are also things to learn at the less successful facilities.
- Above all, be courteous.
- You are responsible for filling in the field exercise questionnaire sheets as best you can. Do not waste the time of the manager or employees by asking them to help you with questionnaires. You will learn more by making your own evaluations. If you cannot possibly answer some of the questions through your own observations—leave them blank.
- Spend at least 1 hour at each field trip location. In my experience, the average investigator who analyzes the facility carefully will spend at least 2 hours while many observers can find plenty of interesting material for a 4 or 5 hour visit—depending upon the location.
- Andmar Press grants the original purchaser of *Make Money Growing Plants, Trees, and Flowers* exception to copyright laws in order to make multiple copies of field exercises. This exception applies only to the personal use of the original owner and specifically does not allow reproduction by any means of additional material in this book.

PRODUCTION FACILITY
FIELD EXERCISE

Suggested observation outline and questionnaire

1. What is the name of this facility?

2. What type of business or combination business is it?

3. What types of ornamental crops are grown here?

4. Can you name some of the more important species of plants being grown at this site?

5. Would you describe the physical location as urban, suburban, or rural?

6. Can you estimate the total size of this facility in square feet or acres?

7. On the separate grid sheet page provided, draw a rough map of the site layout with all buildings and special features.

8. Does this production facility have a retail sales area on site or at another location, or does it market exclusively through wholesale channels?

9. Do you know what the general market area covered by this firm is?

10. How long has this firm been in business?

11. Make a short list of the major items of machinery and vehicles you notice on site.

12. How many employees have you seen on site?

13. Is there a specific area for employees to have break and clean up?

14. Does the site appear to offer reasonably safe conditions for employees and visitors?

15. Is there a centralized work area or does it seem that most work projects are carried on all over the place?

16. Is the entire business site organized and clean?

Somewhat? Disorganized and trashy?

17. Do the crops look healthy and in an appropriate condition so that you would expect consumers to readily purchase them if the price was reasonable?

18. Does this facility appear to mix its own soil or does it purchase bagged soil mix from specialists?

19. Do the outdoor roadways and indoor aisles allow plenty of room for movement of people and crops?

20. Does this facility obtain water from: Wells? Municipal supply? Pond? Stream?

21. Is this the time of year you would expect the production facility to be reasonably busy?

22. How many of this particular type of production facilities are listed in your local phone book yellow pages?

23. What is the most important point you learned from this field exercise?

24. Does this facility have a wholesale list? Take one, if allowed.

SALES FACILITY FIELD EXERCISE

Suggested observation outline and questionnaire

1. What is the name of this facility?

2. What type of business or combination business is it?

3. What are the main types of horticultural crops sold here?

4. Does the retail facility appear to be a chain store

(mass market) type or does it appear to be an independent store operated by an individual, family, or limited number of partners?

5. Is the store located in an urban, suburban, or rural area?

6. On the grid sheet provided, draw a rough map of the facility layout. Be sure to include outdoor sales areas if they are present.

7. Are the displays of plants clean and orderly?

8. Do you feel the horticultural products are displayed properly to accomplish maximum sales?

9. How would you rate the quality of plant material available at this facility? Good, medium, poor?

10. Is there an associated plant production facility on this retail site?

11. Are there plenty of sales people available to help or is this a more-or-less self service facility?

12. Are there plenty of signs to help customers shop?

13. Is everything clearly priced? If prices are listed on a price sheet, take one.

14. Do you feel the varieties of plants offered here for outdoor use are the proper ones for this climatic region?

15. Is there a good choice of plant material?

16. Does it appear that the plant material is being watered and cared for on an appropriate schedule?

17. Have you noticed any plant pests or apparent plant diseases which would cause customers to reject particular plants on sale at this facility?

18. Do the prices for plant material appear to be reasonable considering the quality, selection, and service available at this store?

19. Are there plenty of check out stations for the amount of business being done?

20. Is there plenty of free parking?

21. Is this facility open year-round?

22. Is this the time of year you would expect this facility to be reasonably busy?

23. Does this store offer a publicly stated guarantee policy which you feel is adequate?

24. How long has this store been in operation?

25. How many of this type of facility are doing business in your locality?

26. What is the most important point you have learned from this field exercise?

LANDSCAPE AND CONSERVATION PROJECT FIELD EXERCISE

Suggested observation outline and questionnaire

1. Is this a public (tax supported) or private project?

2. Is the main purpose of this project beautification, or utilitarian (reclamation, playing fields, etc.), or both in combination?

3. Is this project professionally planned and installed or is it done by amateurs?

4. What are the main types of vegetation being utilized for this project (trees, flowers, lawn, etc.)

5. List some of the major plant varieties used in this project.

6. What is the approximate number of square feet or acres included in this project?

7. On the grid sheet page provided, draw a rough map of the project layout. Be sure to distinguish the main physical features and types of vegetation being used.

8. What is the main feature of this project which catches your eye immediately?

9. Are the vegetation and physical features of this project well-maintained?

10. Was this project planned so that it provides beautification on a year-round basis rather than for limited times?

11. How long do you estimate this project has been installed?

INSTITUTIONAL FACILITY FIELD EXERCISE

Suggested observation outline and questionnaire

1. What is the name of this facility?

2. What type of institution is this?

3. What is the main purpose of this facility?

4. List the major features of this facility (buildings,

grounds, growing areas, work areas, etc.).

5. What are the main species or groups of plants grown or displayed here

6. Approximately how many square feet or acres are included in this facility?

7. On the grid sheet page provided, draw a rough map of the project layout.

8. Is this facility tax supported or private?

9. Do many people seem to use this facility?

10. Is this the season you would expect people to visit the facility?

11. Does this facility seem to serve a worth while purpose?

12. Are there any major operational problems you can see at this facility?

SHOWS, MEETINGS, ORGANIZATIONS FIELD EXERCISE

Suggested observation outline and questionnaire

1. What is the name of this show, meeting, or organization?

2. What is its main purpose or objective?

3. Who is participating in this show, meeting, or organization (business people, men, women, age, amateurs, homeowners)?

4. Do the participants seem to be heavily-involved in horticulture? moderately? slightly?

5. Can you think of any ways this show, meeting, or organization might be of significance to commercial horticulture?

6. How many people are present at this show, meeting, or organization?

7. What are the main impressions or facts you gained from observing this show, meeting, or organization?

8. Take any information you can find that might be applicable to your business. Write down helpful prices.

LIBRARY FIELD EXERCISE

Suggested observation outline and questionnaire

1. What is the name of this library?

2. Approximately how many books in the horticulture, gardening, agriculture, and botany sections of this library have some relationship to ornamental horticulture? How many magazines?

3. Give the name of at least one reference guide in which you can find all the published periodicals (magazines) listed which pertain to horticulture and gardening (if you cannot find one, ask the librarian to show you how to locate and use such periodical guides).

4. List the most important type of information which is given about magazines in the periodical guide.

5. Can you think of any other subject areas besides

horticulture, gardening, agriculture, and botany where you might find information in this library which relates to ornamental horticulture?

6. Write the name of at least 2 periodicals or books useful in commercial horticulture which you have found present in the library. Make sure you have examined the general contents of each one carefully.

7. Do the horticultural titles in this library seem up to date (published recently)?

8. Does this library have an interlibrary loan program with major libraries which are more likely to have a greater amount of material related to ornamental horticulture?

9. Do you think this library has an adequate selection of subject matter about ornamental horticulture?

10. If you cannot find appropriate information in this library, what other local facilities are there where you might locate such material?

INTERNET EXERCISE

The Internet is a revolutionary invention which can potentially make unlimited information available to anyone who has access to a computer equipped with a modem. Although the Internet and the World Wide Web are technically separate entities, for the purposes of this discussion the terms are interchangeable. Discovered by physicists, this computer-based information superhighway can, if employed properly, make the gathering of information necessary for success in business easier and more fruitful than ever before. The Internet is a tool which cannot be ignored. Proper navigation of the World Wide Web can enhance the success of your business. By keeping abreast of the latest trends and information in your field of endeavor, you gain the benefit of valuable knowledge, and, often times, the information is free.

There are, however, a few problems with this seemingly miraculous discovery. The major problem is the issue of findability. Due to the tremendous growth of websites and surfers, the information superhighway is cluttered with cul-de-sacs and false exits. In other words, the Internet, increasingly, can be viewed more as a labyrinth than a clearly marked highway. The people responsible for creating the search engines failed to utilize the time tested-methods of categorization employed by librarians; they ignored library science. This was a critical oversight for which there is no quick cure.

Another problem concerning findability and the search engines is the number of search engines and the (for lack of a better term) esoteric means which each engine uses to retrieve documents. There are hundreds of search engines and each one uses a different method of document retrieval. Because there has never been a uniform classification system put into place before web pages are submitted, the result is a mishmash of information which, more often than not, makes the search for specific material (unless the terminology used in the search is decidedly technical or scientific) tedious and time consuming.

There are also the reverse engineers or "hackers" who manipulate search engines by analyzing document retrieval methods. When these reverse engineers or, to use a literary term, deconstructionists, "hack" a search engine, they are able to utilize the data to promote their (or their employers') web sites and pages to the top of that particular search engine. If you are familiar with web surfing, you undoubtedly have experienced a search which yields illogical results. For example, you search the terms "greenhouse and pesticides," and the top 10 results have nothing to do with either of these terms. This is the way of the World Wide Web. As of yet, there is no clear way to deal with this problem. It would take an army of librarians years to classify the documents which already exist on the web, let alone the thousands upon thousands which are added each day.

Still, the World Wide Web can provide a wealth of information if you have the patience to look for it. Carefully choosing the words which will define your search may eliminate a number of false leads. When a search yields poor results, try another combination of words to narrow the field of your search. Navigating the World Wide Web takes cunning and patience. With a little practice, you will soon find that your time is well spent.

Internet Practical

As stated earlier, you can find virtually anything on the World Wide Web. As such, it is important to narrow the search in order to avoid hours of wasted time and eye strain. Since this book is concerned with income opportunities in horticulture, it would prove most useful to begin narrowing the search at this point. Below you are asked to find specific sites concerning horticulture. After successfully completing this lesson, you will be equipped with the necessary skills to help you find all kinds of business information.

On a separate piece of paper, research the topics listed below. Be thorough, the only one you cheat by skimping is yourself.

1. Find the site of your state's Department of Agriculture.

a) Do they offer any services?

b) How can you implement these services into your horticultural enterprise?

c) What kind of information do they provide that could be beneficial (or detrimental) to your proposed operation?

2. Locate the sites of three U.S. Agricultural Extension Offices.

a) How are they the same?

b) How are they different?

3. Find sites providing technical information concerning:

a) Roses.

b) Orchids.

c) Poinsettias.

Did you find conflicting information in the culture of roses? Orchids? Poinsettias?

4. Search for the U.S. Department of Commerce site.

a) Find the Weather Bureau.

b) Analyze weather averages/extremes in your area.

5. Find the Environmental Protection Agency site.

a) Do they offer any services?

b) Do they post regulations which may effect your business?

6. Locate the site of your state's Department of Environmental Quality.

a) Do they offer any services?

b) Do they post regulations that may effect your business?

7. Search for the U.S. Small Business Administration site.

a) Can you find any information which may be beneficial to your proposed operation?

b) Are there any programs in which you might want to enroll in?

8. Find the U.S. Department of Agricultural Statistics site.

a) Analyze crop production schedules.

9. Locate three greenhouse and/or nursery association sites.

a) Is there a local chapter?

b) Is there a state chapter?

c) What benefits would you gain by joining the association?

10. Search for three horticultural trade show sites.

a) What do the trade shows offer?

b) What would you gain by attending each trade show?

11. Find three greenhouse or nursery magazine sites.

a) Which magazines would you consider subscribing to?

b) Why?

Name of Facility_____

Grid sheet for recording layout of facilities visited on field trip. Label vertical and horizontal divisions in appropriate scale (multiples of feet).

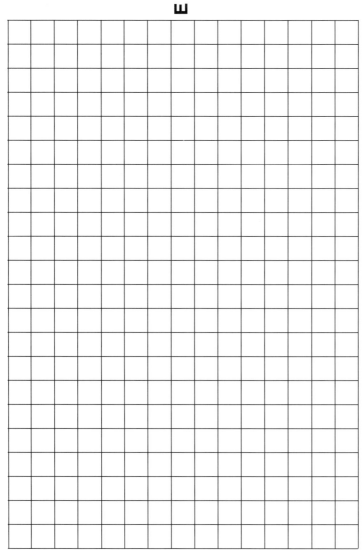

Name of Facility_____

Grid sheet for recording layout of facilities visited on field trip. Label vertical and horizontal divisions in appropriate scale (multiples of feet).

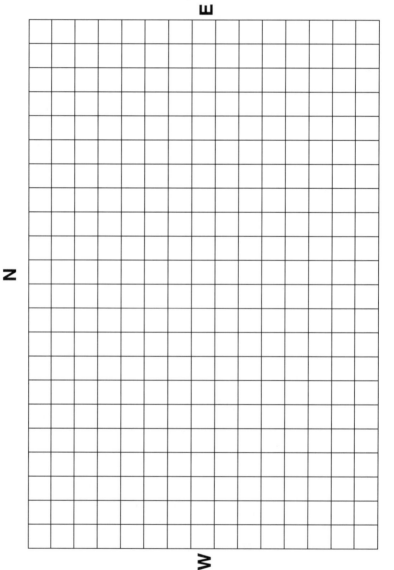

Name of Facility_____

Grid sheet for recording layout of facilities visited on field trip. Label vertical and horizontal divisions in appropriate scale (multiples of feet).

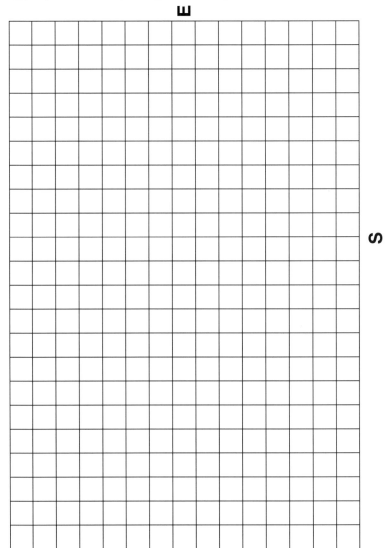

Name of Facility_____

Grid sheet for recording layout of facilities visited on field trip. Label vertical and horizontal divisions in appropriate scale (multiples of feet).

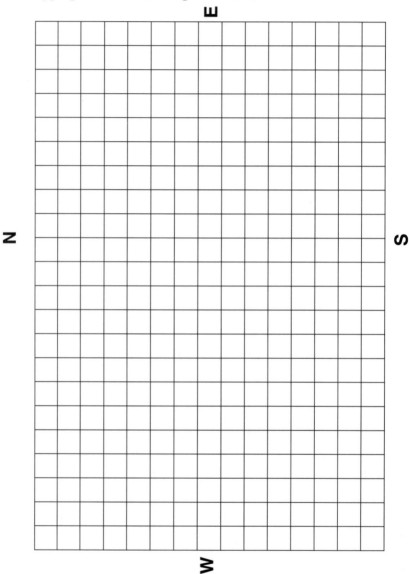

Personal Note from the Author:

Hopefully, this book will help you avoid many of the business errors I have committed throughout the years. Specific information is important, of course, but developing proper thinking habits and concentrating your time upon the most critical aspects of business are more productive than trying to remember numerous facts which could be more easily filed and left out of mind until needed.

The following are some factors which it will pay to keep foremost in mind during the daily routine. Commit them to memory so that they are considered in every business decision.

1. Trial and error are a big part of life, learn from each mistake so that it need not be repeated.

2. Try to arrange your business development so that growth can be completed one logical step at a time without jeopardizing any previous progress.

3. Don't commit major resources to unproven projects. Test them first with carefully planned experimental models.

4. Always evaluate the amount of risk present in every project against the amount of likely gain to be realized.

5. Labor will generally be the largest outlay in any horticultural growing operation. Be sure you control this expense carefully and thoughtfully with long-range planning.

6. Evaluate expense categories carefully to determine which ones deserve the major efforts for control.

7. Don't allow your business to grow helter-skelter. Build definable programs which fit together logically and which run more-or-less automatically once perfected. Otherwise, you will be "reinventing the wheel" every day as decisions must be made.

Chapter 10

SELLING AT A PROFIT

It is surprising that many horticultural growers spend less than a few hours every year planning how to market their crops. They toil countless hours trying to make their plants the best available and then neglect to implement even elementary marketing efforts to insure the crop is sold at a good profit. To my mind, there is nothing more disheartening than seeing plants die on the shelf for lack of a buyer. A well-conceived and realistic sales plan should be designed for each crop before any production takes place.

Although growing plants is the first love of any horticulturist, our concern in this book is not only with growing plants, but also with selling them at a profit. The growing and selling equation cannot be said to have a side which is more important. Each time you modify one side of the equation, the other side also changes. The key objective of a horticultural business is to coordinate production with sales in order to achieve the maximum profits possible. This happy outcome does not happen without effort.

The old adage that all you have to do is build a better mousetrap to have people beat a path to your door is simply not true in today's world. People expect you to make your products conveniently available to them, both in location and presentation. They also expect you to let them know how to use the product and what its advantages and disadvantages are. In short, they expect you to actively sell the product to them, not simply make it available.

There are many ingredients in a sales recipe for profitable business operation. Forget the idea that the act of selling merchandise is comprised only of the presentation a sales person gives to the customers. The sales program of your company is affected by every action you take and every action you don't take. Your method of growing plants, location, pricing structure, and many more factors will affect every sale. Topics which should be considered whenever a sales program is being constructed will now be explored.

LOCATION

The success or failure of a business often hinges upon its physical location. In general, location is a more critical factor if you plan to sell at retail directly to the public. While location is important to a wholesale business for a variety of reasons, it does not often greatly affect access to the product by potential wholesale customers.

Obviously, if we all had our choice of location without regard to cost or availability, there would be no problem. Everyone would choose the very best. This is seldom the case in the real world since we must balance the favorable attributes of a location with the negative aspects — such as price. A good location will cost more to rent or buy. Only in exceptional circumstances will you encounter the lucky situation where an excellent business location can be purchased at a bargain price.

The type of location needed for a horticultural business depends upon many factors. The differences between wholesale and retail have already been mentioned. A wholesale grower may require access to irrigation water, good soil, and roads adequate for heavy trucks while a retail florist would need none of these. A retail florist who plans on doing 90% phone business does not require a high traffic location while a florist who concentrates on cash and carry walk-in customers needs to be where the people are.

Exactly what type of business you plan to operate must be carefully analyzed before choosing a location. Alternatively, if there is only one possible location, you must plan a business which has a good chance of success in that spot.

The place you begin business is often the same spot you will terminate commercial activities many years later. If 20 or 30 years are spent working in a location, doesn't it make sense to choose this environment carefully? Even a small difference in suitability can assume large proportions when multiplied by the number of hours you will spend at the workplace over a 20-year span. Convenience is not the only factor. Think about the amount of sales and profits which will be sacrificed in the same time frame if only 10% of total sales is lost because you selected a poor location. A well-established small retail nursery or greenhouse might have gross sales in 2000 of $500,000 per year. Ten percent of this figure for 20 years would amount to $1,000,000 in lost sales. This is a high price to pay for not taking the time

Selling At A Profit

Table 12

Sample property attribute valuation for 3 tree nursery sites based upon zero (0) for lowest valued property in attribute category. Example: if all properties are of equal estimated value in an attribute category, they are all at 0. Estimated valuation of attribute category is not directly related to actual total price as stated in real estate offer. Assume all 3 properties' asking price is equal.

Location attributes evaluated	Relative Value of Attributes		
	Location A	Location B	Location C
Improvements	$10,000	$0 (unimproved)	$15,000
Utilities available	10,000	0 (none)	10,000
Parking	0	0 (none)	0
Roads, highways	10,000	0 (none)	5,000
Zoning classification	10,000	0 (none)	10,000
Access to customer base	10,000	0	5,000
Convenience to owner	0	10,000	0
Soil quality	0	10,000	0
Topography	0	0	0
Irrigation water	0	10,000	0
Environmental liabilities	1,000	2,000	0
Quality surroundings	0	5,000	0
Relative value of attributes for total business location	$51,000	$37,000	$45,000

It is easy to see that when considering only the attributes evaluated, location A is the most valuable. Unless it is lacking in an attribute that is critical (cannot do without), it would be the logical choice for purchase since all 3 properties have the same asking price.

to choose a business location carefully.

Of course, the best spots cost more money to buy. No one is going to give you the perfect location out of the goodness of their heart. The purchase price must be balanced against potential benefits received. Sometimes the most expensive location is not the best overall choice because it may not generate enough extra income to justify the higher price.

Once several locations are found which seem appropriate for the proposed business, draw up a written comparison sheet which outlines the benefits and drawbacks of each. Then assign a dollar value to every factor in the list and add up the totals. It is amazing how often this process shows clearly which choice offers the best value. However, sometimes it won't work so well, and you will have to rely upon personal preferences to make the final selection. Professional real estate appraisers may be able to help in site selection, but they are unlikely to be knowledgeable about the specialized needs of a horticultural business.

Considering the massive impact a poor business location can have on your financial well being, it is wiser to choose a slightly better location than necessary rather than one which proves to be inadequate. It is often prudent to postpone any long term location commitments until you have the experience to choose wisely.

WHAT ARE YOU ARE SELLING AND TO WHOM

Almost every new business person suffers an identity crisis. It takes time and practical experience to learn exactly what you are selling and who your customers are. This statement may sound naive to some readers. They might say "I will sell anything to anyone who wants to buy it." This is about the broadest statement which could be made, and, upon reflection, the inadequacy of it will become obvious. Certainly you do not intend to sell washing machines or automobiles to preschool children at your horticultural business. You plan to sell horticulturally-related merchandise to a predominately adult clientele. Even this more narrowly defined mission will need further focus in order to provide an exact understanding of your commercial objectives.

The point to be made is this: no business can successfully handle all types of merchandise and sell to all groups of people. The type of merchandise to be sold and the clientele to whom it will be sold must be carefully defined so that the business can concentrate upon a realistically obtainable objective rather than wasting effort trying to please everyone. Even within the horticultural field or within specific specialties, you will need to define exactly what it is your business does and who makes up its customer base.

An example may clear this topic up a bit. Suppose you open a retail greenhouse and find from experience that spring garden plants, potted flowers, and indoor foliage plants comprise a profitable and well-integrated combination of products. These products are sold primarily to middle class people who stay home and garden a lot, either indoors or outdoors. Each day as you drive to the greenhouse for work, you notice a nearby fancy flower shop with lots of ritzy customers in Cadillacs going in and out. Such activity indicates that this flower shop is doing a land office business, so you then decide to set up a similar shop at your greenhouse. Is this a good decision? Probably not!

Your present gardening customers and the Cadillac crowd may not prove to be a compatible mixture. It is difficult to run a fancy flower shop amidst the dirt and fertilizer piles of a garden store. Furthermore, the busy season for garden plants conflicts with the largest cut flower occasion — Mother's Day. You would have to neglect one or the other parts of your business during that period. Serving two masters is an invitation for conflict.

Determining the general type of product or service which will be sold is the first major merchandising decision. Remember, concentrate on something you truly enjoy and which offers the prospect of reasonable profits. The highest profit items may grow old if you don't enjoy the work. Conversely, poor profits take the fun out of life. The next logical step is to find out who the most profitable customers for that product might be. Will they be wholesale or retail, and, if they are retail, should you concentrate sales promotions upon rich or poor, young or old?

With so much competition from chain stores nowadays, it is often more logical to concentrate in products or services which they have a hard time merchandising properly — don't go head-to-head with them on easily handled items like tools, bark chips, hoses, etc.

Once the customer base has been defined, you may have to return attention to the product and make alterations in the production process so that the product is tailored more closely to the exact customer audience defined.

It is not easy to find your most profitable and comfortable niche in the business world. A lot of trial and error is involved, and it is next to impossible to hit the bull's-eye with the first try. A business is much easier to operate and more profitable once you are clearly focused upon only those objectives which contribute meaningfully to success. Many business persons behave like impatient teenagers who cannot concentrate on a limited number of realistic goals — they want to do everything right now. Once a successful method of operation has been achieved, don't meddle with it needlessly. Let the customers tell you what they want by allowing them to choose from test presentations, then change only if the figures from a test are positive.

HOW TO REACH CUSTOMERS

When you have determined the approximate clientele of your new business, it is essential to find an economical means of bringing these potential customers into contact with your product. This is a key element of business success, and it is not as easy to achieve as it might seem.

There are many ways of bringing product and customer together. Each method has its own particular usefulness, depending upon the circumstances which prevail. Some of the methods will be outlined below, along with comments about their effectiveness and other important characteristics.

Interaction of location with other factors

We have mentioned this topic several times previously and need not to pursue it further except to inquire how it interacts with other means of attracting customers.

A well-manicured lawn and displays of garden merchandise outdoors make this greenhouse a peaceful haven even though it is easily accessed from a main business thoroughfare.

Obviously, your business location is a major factor in determining how many and what kind of customer will visit. Not only the physical location, but also the condition, quality, and other characteristics of the premises are important.

Most businesses will benefit from a location which has very high vehicle traffic only if it offers an opportunity for motorists to slow down and exit the main street. Even if your customers can reach your location easily, they will not stay unless there is plenty of free off-street parking.

A horticultural-oriented business is normally dealing in merchandise which the customer hopes will add some beauty, tranquility, and spiritual meaning to his or her life. Dirty, noisy, blacktop parking lots make it difficult

The inside atmosphere of a similar retail greenhouse is no less inviting, rewarding the curious shopper with uncommon pleasures.

for trees and flowers to implant their important psychological messages into the customers minds.

If a business location is not perfect in terms of exposure and accessibility, often it can be upgraded in total drawing power by installing a landscape which is especially inviting to horticulturists. A tasteful landscape setting is often the most cost-effective means of presenting horticultural products for sale. You can do the work yourself and obtain the necessary plants and materials through wholesale channels.

Other methods of attracting and influencing customers will prove largely ineffective and uneconomical if the business location is unsuitable for one reason or another.

Customers who are drawn to your location by costly newspaper advertisements may be driven away if they can't park with ease or if the store looks run down. A super location with high quality improvements may allow you to spend somewhat less on alternate methods of attracting customers.

Conventional advertising

Now we turn to the means of attracting and persuading customers which undoubtedly is most often thought of whenever the word selling is employed. In today's world, selling is almost equivalent in our minds with advertising. Advertising is an immense field and is the keystone which links products and services with the consumer.

Everyone seems to hold advertising with some disregard, but even the most vehement detractors make use of its services daily. Almost any action which brings the customer into association with a product or service could be termed advertising. However, we will limit our discussion to those visual and auditory media which the ordinary person would consider falling under this classification.

Television, newspapers, magazines, radio, billboards, direct mail, point of sales aids, signs, and product enclosures are only the better known methods of advertising. Every conceivable means of communicating with and influencing customers has been utilized by businesses.

You will not discover any new bombshell means of advertising a horticultural business, but you can make wise choices from existing advertising avenues.

Perhaps no other aspect of operating a business is less understood and more wasteful of money than is advertising. Everyone does some advertising just because it seems to be the thing to do. And, if a business is in trouble, the thought that often pops into mind is "we need to do more advertising."

The reason that general advertising is often such a waste of money is because it is very difficult to accurately measure its effectiveness. I have placed hundreds of advertisements over the years for horticultural products and mail order books — in order to assure that my money is not wasted, I focus upon one important rule: always structure advertising efforts so that some means of measuring effectiveness is present. This is not easy to accomplish. Various tools such as coupons and contests for prizes can be used to at least measure immediate response. Over the longer term, it may be possible to correlate sales volume with advertising efforts.

In addition to measuring response as carefully as possible, you can save money by observing some time-tested rules of thumb when deciding where and how to spend your advertising budget. Target an audience by using the medium which reaches your customer base most economically. Local newspapers are generally the most cost effective means of advertising in a smaller town. In large population centers, this is not the case unless you have multiple outlets in most sections of the city. Television may be a glamorous way to reach customers, but it is usually too expensive for small, local merchants to use effectively.

Advertising space is expensive and almost every advertiser could make their budget go further by structuring messages to produce the greatest effect in the least possible space. Do not try to impress people by running larger advertisements than absolutely necessary. Take pride in your ability to get the message across as briefly as possible.

General Motors may have the financial resources to simply advertise their name, but small merchants must attract customers with the promise of specific benefits. If your product is attractively priced, be sure the price is conspicuously mentioned in the advertisements. If quality and selection are your strong points, try to advertise specific examples of these facts rather than simply using the lifeless words "quality and selection." In the simple advertisement you will see reproduced shortly, each of the specific benefits are clearly spelled out.

Most small business persons are not advertising experts. They do not possess any special talent for creating extraordinarily powerful advertisements. Studying basic advertising strategies and techniques in a few good books will help you become conversant in the subject, and, even if you don't design your own ads, it will help you evaluate the performance of those who do the job for you.

Representatives of the local advertising media will be glad to help you design ads if you are doing business with them. However, these people have hundreds of customers, and they cannot be expected to come up with a work of art for each account. They also know very little about your business needs and strategies. It is up to you to make sure the advertising they design is suitable for your purposes. They will usually try to sell you more than you can afford or need. Don't be impressed by their sales pitch, buy only what you need.

Ask for special packages and prices! Only a fool pays the first price an advertising representative quotes. It is like buying a car: there is always a better price if you are willing to wait — and if you ask.

It is difficult to say how much you should spend on all forms of advertising. Every business has such varying needs and circumstances. Once a business is functioning normally without the need to announce business openings or to contact the initial customer base, it is likely that the total advertising budget for a retail store should not exceed 4-5% of sales. If you have an extremely good location, less than this might be budgeted for advertising while a poor location might require a larger expenditure.

Special types of horticultural businesses may allocate a good deal more, or less, to advertising: some wholesale growers can do a good business with no formal advertising at all while a firm specializing in mail order plants might conceivably spend 50% of sales revenues on advertising.

The 4-5% figure mentioned above should be interpreted to include all outlays for advertising, not just the more obvious expenses for such things as radio commercials or newspaper spots.

There are commercial advertising agencies who can manage your advertising efforts. As in any other field, there are good agencies and poor ones. Don't let anyone handle advertising without your personal approval of major aspects. Whatever they do should be examined to make sure it is sensible. Most likely, an established advertising agency will not be interested in your account anyway. It won't be big enough to make them a good profit.

Once you find a few ads that work, put them in a file and use them each year as the occasion dictates.

Customers don't study them like you do, so it doesn't hurt to save time by repeating the same ad several years.

My personal opinion is that small businesses should depend as much as possible upon avenues other than conventional advertising to attract customers. Conventional advertising is expensive, and it is difficult to determine its effectiveness. The seasonal nature of most horticultural businesses dictates that a great majority of advertising expenditures be made in a short amount of time: when you have lots of merchandise and when people have an active desire for the product. Advertising poinsettias in July is a futile exercise.

Most of the advertising you do should be directed at specific events, holidays, or special sales. This will ensure that plenty of merchandise is available and that people will be interested; it also helps evaluate ad effectiveness to some extent. Running special sales or coupon ads is perhaps the only reasonably accurate way to measure response.

At carefully selected times, it is good to run a small ad with tremendous bargains for the customer. A half-price sale will bring lots of business with only a small advertising expense, and it is easy to tell if you are getting response. A 10% off sale will not draw as many customers and will likely require more ad space to draw attention. The 10% off promotion may be so weak as to make it difficult to tell whether or not it was effective in drawing additional customers. If this happens, you cannot draw any conclusions about merchandise desirability or advertising medium suitability.

Many business people try to be creative and run cute or funny advertisements. This is a mistake unless you are in the business of being a comedian. Customers are

This advertisement combines many excellent characteristics: simple and easy to understand, appeal to local pride, specific benefits to customers, promises a large selection. A small ad with big impact, it draws crowds year after year. Notice the distinctive upper logo which has been in use for over 30 years. Provides instant name recognition for superior quality products.

interested in the benefits your product will provide them — not in being entertained.

Advertising will likely be one part of business that you understand the least and which is less predictable in terms of results. You may never reach any accurate conclusions about exactly how it affects business. In this type of situation, the best course is caution. Would you commit a lot of money to another project if you had no idea how it would work? Spend your advertising dollars first on those areas where you can be reasonably certain of effective results.

Word of mouth

Satisfied customers are the lifeblood of any business. They will spread the good word far and wide. Customer goodwill is the best and most economical type of advertising your firm can utilize.

In the horticultural field, a good business reputation is like money in the bank. Reputation is so important in horticultural products and services because the difference in quality between plants and services are not often readily apparent at the time of purchase. Customers rely upon the integrity of the seller to a large degree.

This is the central reason why independent horticultural businesses have been able to compete successfully against major national chain stores. Consumers willingly pay a higher price at independent garden stores if they believe the quality and service are better. A horticultural firm must guard its reputation for superior products and fair customer treatment with its very life. Being in business is a long term project; even though being fair to the customer may cost you money in a specific

A simple sign lets customers know the name of plants and the essentials of good care. Signs save a lot of time while letting people know that your business operation has professional knowledge available.

situation, that satisfied customer will be back many times in the future (and probably with a friend who will also buy something).

A liberal guarantee policy which protects the purchaser's interests is the first step toward customer satisfaction. Reliability and merchant goodwill must be a further part of the guarantee. Customers will not regard your guarantee as being worth much if it has not been honored cheerfully in the past.

Guarantees are not effective unless they represent a sound product or service which is offered by a firm with acknowledged expertise in the field. The purpose of a guarantee is to ensure that isolated chance events or lapses in quality will not be at the customer's expense. Guarantees cannot take the place of good merchandise.

Not a good deal more needs to be said concerning how a business builds a sound reputation for quality products and knowledgeable service. Expertise comes only with hard work and study. Trust will result by following the old proverb "do to others as you would have them do to you."

No matter what other methods may be employed to promote your business, word-of -mouth will eventually be the main avenue by which new customers are acquired. Study after study has shown that if a person does not already have a favorite place to purchase horticultural goods, their choice is dictated by the recommendation of an acquaintance or family member. Time passes quickly, and you will be surprised how fast a business can grow through referrals; it works just like a chain letter.

Considering that word-of-mouth costs you nothing and is by far the most effective marketing tool available, doesn't it make sense that you should cultivate it to the fullest extent possible before extending customer contact efforts into more expensive and less fruitful avenues?

Face to face contact

The owner and perhaps a few key employees provide the principle image which customers have of a firm. It is vitally important that this image be one which works to the benefit of the company. Customers like to deal with a real person when they need assistance. You can help the business immeasurably by thinking carefully about the image you and your employees should present during customer contact. If you act as knowledgeable and courteous professionals, a tremendous advantage will be gained over competitors who cannot act or fail to act in this manner.

As was stressed previously, a successful horticultural company must have the trust of its clientele. Many of the products and services you sell will not initially appear to the customer as being different from inferior look alikes. How can a customer tell live seed from dead seed or fresh cut flowers from ones that are three days older? People must have confidence in your description of the merchandise. Any misrepresentations will eventually result in less business.

The quality of information given out is also an important ingredient of business success. Most purchasers of horticultural products need advice from time to time. While you cannot be expected to know the solutions to all the problems at all times, your advice must be basically correct and practical for the customer to utilize. Your knowledge of horticulture must be communicated in a way that is easy to understand. Remember, the people you are dealing with are, for the most part, unfamiliar with specialized terminology and procedures. Present yourself as an expert, but not as one who talks down to listeners.

The art of personal contact and personalized selling is not a talent possessed in equal degree by everyone. You may not naturally be very good at it, but you can learn how to perform the essential points in at least an acceptable manner. Business owners and managers are obligated to learn how to effectively interact with other people.

Uncooperative and rude salespeople can poison your business image quickly. Monitor the sales force regularly and make adjustments right away if necessary. It is not a pleasant task to fire someone, but losing your business is even more unpleasant. Perhaps a person who is not "cut out" for sales may do a much better job in the production phases of the operation.

Special promotions

No single happening or event in the sales program will likely cause a significant change in how successful your company is. Success will result from numerous marketing decisions and actions taken over a period of time. However, it is possible to initiate specific marketing objectives by utilizing extraordinary methods which are not normally effective when employed on a regular basis.

Under this category, I am grouping such events as grand openings, anniversaries, public holidays or events, close out sales, special learning opportunities, and almost any other happening which does not take place with any great degree of frequency. The horticultural industry is fortunate in having many special events during each year which increases public awareness of your products. Most of these special days are associated with the floral segment of horticulture, but such events as Arbor Day, Earth Day, and local beautification projects are also helpful in promoting horticulturally-based business.

We are especially blessed with that one great event each year which propels the public into a frenzy (even if short-lived) of fertilizing, cultivating, and planting activity: Spring!

Special promotions, by their very nature, must not be overused if they are to be effective. Since they cannot be employed frequently, any associated promotional effort should be planned carefully so as not to waste the opportunity.

Community interaction

On the political and business news scene, we often hear of "the old boy network." In many cases, this phenomenon is spoken of with distaste, as perhaps a practice which verges on the unethical. Yet, each one of us probably employs similar tactics to promote our personal interests in everyday life. It is simply a part of human nature to prefer dealing with people you know (at least if your knowledge is favorable), and to help those who show an inclination to help you.

I have mentioned a number of times how important it is to have the customer's trust when you are selling horticultural products. This trust may be cultivated in many different ways, but the most effective means (and by far the least expensive) is to be known personally in a favorable light by a large number of your potential customers. People may get to know you strictly through interaction at the business site, or they may know you through personal or associative contact which occurs as part of daily life in the community. Needless to say, trust based upon the latter type of knowledge is considered more reliable because it has no direct connection with your personal gain.

Utilizing your personal community-based reputation as a business asset is no sin. If your reputation was bad, no one would consider it improper to avoid doing business with you. Why should the reverse not be acceptable? If you enjoy community involvement, there is no better long term means of acquiring substantial goodwill for your business than to draw upon the positive image such participation can help develop.

Every town has a group of intensely avid gardeners and horticulture enthusiasts. It is important to cultivate good relations with these people since they greatly influence the general horticultural atmosphere. Each of them is likely to be looked up to as an advisor by several less experienced gardeners. A recommendation of your business by one of these local experts is sure to result in additional sales.

Trade associations and fairs

Wholesale producers of horticultural goods should investigate the advantages which trade associations and trade fairs can lend to their selling efforts. These avenues of business promotion are important in particular circumstances within the horticultural industry, but will not likely benefit you greatly as long as you have a very small business.

Trade shows are definitely a good means for businesses to find new types of merchandise to sell, but exhibiting to sell products at these shows is quite expensive. Only those who have a large amount of appropriate product to sell will find the expense justified.

RELATIONSHIPS OF PRODUCTS TO PERCEPTIONS OF VALUE

Business managers are always concerned about the proper price to charge for different merchandise. Some conventional pricing structures used in the horticultural trade will be discussed, but first I would like to deal with a more-or-less philosophical question which underlies the entire matter of price.

Many people have a vague feeling that prices of goods and services should bear some relationship to the actual physical utility of these items. Of course, only a moment of reflection will be sufficient for you to realize that this is not the case in the real world. In fact, the reverse is often true! What physical purpose does a perfect diamond or a painting by Michelangelo serve for the common man? Yet the price of these items is dear.

The point is this: your job as a manger of a business is not to assign values to goods and services, rather it is to determine what price represents the most monetarily profitable equilibrium between supply and demand. The market will set the price; your task is to find out what that price is.

Everyone who is in business for any length of time eventually has this fact forced upon them, whether they like it or not. I hope you accept it sooner rather than later. Doing so will make will make your job easier and business more profitable. In the commercial world, there are no absolute philosophical values for merchandise. It is worth exactly what the customer will pay for it — no more, no less.

Determining how much the customer will pay, although easier than dealing with philosophical problems, is no simple task. With most established products it is accomplished by observing what price the same type of merchandise commonly sells for under similar circumstances. Adjustments of course must be made for details such as quality, additional services rendered, and the like. Basically, it is a game of monkey see, monkey do. One thing should be kept in mind: you (the merchant) have price in mind constantly while the customer seldom thinks about your prices — he or she is not likely to consider this the most important reason for a purchase in most cases. This fact has been proven time after time by horticultural industry surveys.

When a product or service is sufficiently different from previously existing ones, no reasonable conclusions can be made as to what price customers will pay for it. In this case, the intelligent way of determining the most profitable price is to test different price levels on a trial basis. This assignment is rather difficult to accomplish in a small business, but the effort must be made in order to have any factual knowledge about the price. Larger companies often perform extensive pricing tests which can determine the most profitable price in a very exact manner.

The small business manager must often use rather imprecise methods to determine the most profitable prices. As long as the methods employed have a logical basis and are consistent with one another, they will serve better than wild guesses. Two rules of thumb which I use in pricing are: if more merchandise is being sold than should reasonably be expected, the price is too low; and if you never hear a customer complain about the price being too high, then it is too low.

Plant products are very difficult to assign precise values. This makes your job harder but also potentially more profitable! If you can convince consumers that your trees and shrubs and flowers are a better value than those at discount stores, then the next step is to find out how much more the average customer is willing to pay for higher quality. This can be done with fair accuracy by pricing a particular item at one level for a week and then testing sales the next week at a different price level. This is far from a perfect test since natural demand may vary week from week, but it will give a reasonable indication if you carefully compare results while factoring in such variables as weather and total merchandise sales during the test period. Naturally, you should confirm results with one or more additional tests after the first one.

PRICING AND PROFIT

Although allowing the market to determine prices is preferable to alternative methods, the interplay of market forces requires a certain amount of time to manifest itself adequately. In some cases, it may be extremely difficult to arrive at any reasonably accurate conclusions from observing the results of market forces. For both of these reasons, merchandise and service prices are often set by rather arbitrary but practically useful methods. As long as you keep in mind that these alternative methods are subject to modification whenever market forces yield a more fundamentally sound pricing structure, there is no reason not to employ them for the sake of convenience.

One means of setting prices is by using "price levels." These levels, such as $4.95, $9.95, and on up have no relation to actual value of the product but may be useful to employ when other pricing formulas yield an approximate price. For example, if you wish to double the wholesale cost of $2.30 for an item, it may prove wisest to price it at $4.95 since this is often considered a critical price level (just under $5). In other words, it makes no difference to most customers whether the price is $4.60 or $4.95 since they consider the effective price to be $5.

Merchants often set prices by using a predetermined "mark up" for merchandise. In some cases, the mark up results from an actual analysis of revenues and expenses involved in completing a transaction. In other cases, mark up results from utilizing certain formulas which have attained some degree of popular acceptance within the industry. These formulas are regarded as useful because over time and in many situations they have proven to yield an adequate profit margin for business to prosper.

There is sometimes a good deal of confusion about how to express mark ups in mathematical terms. For example: doubling the production cost or the wholesale cost to arrive at a retail price is often referred to as a 50% mark up. In my estimation, it would be more logical to call this a 100% mark up. Of course, the confusion arises because one person thinks in terms of wholesale price while the retail price forms the basis of another person's calculations. I will express mark up in terms of a number used to multiply the wholesale price.

Basing prices on an analysis of actual costs and revenues involved in transactions has the benefit of assuring that the business will not lose money by selling at a particular price (at least if the selling price is set somewhat above wholesale or production costs). It has the disadvantage of not having a basis in supply and demand market forces.

Conventional mark up formulas have exactly the opposite advantages and disadvantages. They do take some small account of market forces since most other competing businesses are using similar formulas and presumably have found that the formula contains, in part, some approximation of the most profitable market price for that type of product. There is, however, no guarantee that the general formulas will yield profitable prices in specific circumstances or for specific businesses. Only an actual analysis of the transaction can provide this information.

In the horticultural industry, there are some very general rules of thumb for pricing which seem to work reasonably well. These pricing formulas are used mainly by independent stores rather than by volume outlets, and they generally assume that freight costs have already been added onto a base price to arrive at a wholesale cost for the product.

Hard goods such as fertilizers, tools, and insecticides usually are sold at retail for about double the wholesale costs. Big ticket items like garden tractors may have a much smaller, mark up. Trees, plants, and flowers are often sold at three times the wholesale price if considerable advisory service and a guarantee are included with the sale. These perishable items command more or less price as the service provided goes up or down. Of course, the degree of service is not the only factor which lends variation to prices, but it is one of the major items.

Newcomers to business often fail to adequately charge for all the special help given with most sales. Eventually, they find that all these small services add up to a significant drain upon their time and profit margin. In a few cases, business owners place an exaggerated value upon their expertise and overcharge for services. You must analyze the situation carefully and try to arrive at a realistic appraisal of proper charges. Personally, I have seldom regretted raising prices, but there have been many occasions when I lost significant income by not charging enough.

It may seem to some readers that a few percent one way or the other in pricing policy should not have a major impact upon business success. Nothing could be further from the truth. A small percentage change in prices often multiplies the profit percentage many times. Table 13 shows the relationship between selling price and profit for potted geranium plants sold by a greenhouse.

These figures illustrate that only a small change in selling price can effect profits tremendously. This is why you must be extremely careful when pricing policies are formulated. Profit margins often rise greatly in response to only small increases in selling price and vice-versa. The changes in profit have been dramatized by illustrating what takes place at profit levels near the break-even point. This area is where price changes will show the greatest effect on profits. You should first concentrate upon fine-tuning prices on major merchandise lines; this is where most of the extra profit can be made. Let less important items wait until last.

The relationship between prices, profits, and volume of merchandise sold are not so well understood by some business people. It seems that there is a near universal tendency among small business managers to speculate on how many more units of a particular product they could sell if they lowered prices. I suppose all of us small fish long to become big fish. Everyone wants to expand. Unfortunately, some small businesses become less successful as they grow because they sacrifice profits for the sake of sales volume. Table 14 provides a look at what happens to total profits at different per unit profit margins when a specific number of units is sold.

It becomes apparent from these figures that total profits can fall quickly as selling price is decreased to entice customers. Eventually, we must expect that decreases in price would no longer result in increased volume because the market is saturated with product.

Table 14 is greatly simplified and relies upon volume figures which are only educated assumptions, but I believe that the general picture revealed is essentially valid. It is true that the wholesale purchase price or the cost of production would likely decrease slightly as the volume of sales went up, but eventually this figure would remain static or change very little. The only thing small wholesale purchase price changes would modify is the point at which increases in volume became less and less profitable.

The two examples point out the perils a business faces when selling prices are modified in response to any market stimulus, and, in particular, when prices are lowered to initiate an increase in sales volume. Lowering prices may be a sound decision for any number of reasons, but there is a large risk that the change may cause an unexpectedly large profit decline.

Tables 13 and 14 also show that pricing variations do not have the same effect under all business conditions.

Price alterations must not be considered as isolated actions. Their effect will be felt in every aspect of your business. These interrelationships demand that each major segment of business operation be examined for possible reactions to proposed changes.

Standardized mark up formulas serve only as aids in establishing a beginning price for merchandise. With

Table 13

Relationship of retail geranium plant prices to profit percentages.

Wholesale price or cost of production	Retail selling price	Total retail gross profit margin	% change in retail price from previous price	% change in profit from previous price
$1.50	$1.55	$0.05	0	0
1.50	1.60	0.10	3.22	100
1.50	1.65	0.15	3.13	50
1.50	1.70	0.20	3.03	33.33
1.50	1.75	0.25	2.94	25
1.50	1.80	0.30	2.86	20
1.50	1.85	0.35	2.78	16.67
1.50	1.90	0.40	2.70	14.29
1.50	1.95	0.45	2.63	12.5
1.50	2.00	0.50	2.56	11.1
1.50	2.05	0.55	2.50	10
1.50	2.10	0.60	2.44	9.09
1.50	2.15	0.65	2.38	8.33
1.50	2.20	0.70	2.33	7.69
1.50	2.25	0.75	2.27	7.14

Table 14

Total profits resulting from sales of geranium plants at different volume and retail price.

Wholesale price	Retail selling price	Per plant gross profit margin	Number of units sold	Total profits
$1.50	$3.00	$1.50	1000	$1,500
1.50	2.25	0.75	2000	1,500
1.50	1.65	0.15	4000	600
1.50	1.55	0.05	5000	250

experience, you will find that certain products sell well at even higher mark ups than normal while some products must be sold at lower mark ups in order to keep them moving along. There is nothing unusual about this situation; it is simply the market telling you that you must modify prices according to the customers needs and preferences.

Some merchants refuse to handle items which, after trial, they find cannot be sold for the accustomed mark up. On the other hand, I have never seen a store manager who declined to handle products that could be sold for higher than normal mark ups. The most realistic approach is to accept higher and lower mark ups as a part of life. As long as the lower mark up item is not actually losing money, it is difficult to justify not selling it if it meets other suitable criteria for your business. Handling merchandise which loses money is another story; there must be an extremely good reason to enter this territory. Even "loss leaders" offered by chain stores are seldom sold at an actual loss.

ESTABLISHMENT OF WHOLESALE PRICES

The pricing discussion we have just been over referred mainly to retail situations. Obviously, wholesale growers of horticultural crops face a somewhat different situation. Although it is possible for wholesalers to use some type of mark up formulas, they must first determine their costs of producing certain crops.

Basically, a wholesale grower adds up all the direct costs of growing a particular plant and then assigns additional overhead expenses to the plant in order to arrive at the total production cost. A wholesale price is then calculated by adding the desired profit level onto production costs.

Several variations in method are often used to determine total production costs. The personal preference of growers often determines the exact method used, but certain conventional procedures are more common in one specialty area than in another. The amount of time and labor it takes to grow a crop and the space occupied are usually the critical factors which determine production costs. *The Greenhouse and Nursery Handbook* provides a detailed explanation of how to calculate wholesale prices.

ADDITIONAL PRICING CONSIDERATIONS

Your success in horticultural business will depend to a great degree upon how well you understand and apply pricing factors. The short space I have devoted to this topic does not do justice to its importance, only some of the more basic considerations have been touched upon. If you start a business, it will be necessary to delve more deeply into this subject. Books, magazines, seminars, and personal observations are the main sources of information which you can utilize. There are many technical factors about pricing which can be picked up through study, it is not necessary to learn everything through the school of hard knocks.

A final observation should be emphasized concerning a profitable operation: Many people in horticultural business are so terrified of having a few items left unsold that they consistently undergrow or underorder. These people will never know how much they could sell if they had plenty of merchandise. I prefer to carefully lean towards having a slight excess of product — this way you are taking full advantage of the market. Additionally, your hard won customers need not visit a competitor to obtain their needs. It is possible the customer might permanently switch allegiance. Remember: you can't sell what you don't have.

Table 15
Possible places to sell plants.

Retail

1. Traditional retail store.
2. Job racking: Providing a particular line of merchandise to a retail store and, within certain guidelines, manage the display, product, and merchandising as if that particular area is your own small retail store.
3. Farmers markets, craft fairs.
4. Off the truck: Renting a good spot and selling right off the truck.
5. Landscaping.
6. Mail order.

Wholesale

1. To retailers.
2. To landscapers.
3. To other wholesalers.
4. To institutions (hospitals, large corporations).
5. To government (military bases, highway departments).
6. To colleges and universities.
7. To malls, amusement parks, and large businesses.
8. To group living centers (retirement centers, condos).
9. To cemeteries.
10. To parks departments.

Personal Note from the Author:
There is one aspect of horticultural marketing over which no one has control: the weather. It is one of the largest determinants (particularly for spring selling) of whether or not horticultural businesses will have a good year. Fortunately, the weather effects everyone in a local area pretty much the same; no one has an advantage in this regard.

You can plan for weather factors and often gain a competitive advantage by devising specific strategies to make it work for you instead of against.

A personal example is my decision years ago to de-emphasize early spring selling efforts in favor of late spring and early summer promotion. Early spring weather in my area is just too unpredictable to base any actual plans upon. The climate only a few weeks later becomes more predictably mild and suitable for selling, thus allowing us to make reliable production estimates for crops.

Sure, we miss a few early spring sales, but the experienced gardeners we are marketing to have long ago learned to wait until proper weather for planting — they know we will have all their needs when the time arrives.

Chapter 11

THE INGREDIENTS FOR BUSINESS SUCCESS

The topics I wish to cover in this chapter are many and can often be expressed sufficiently in a few words. I believe a short presentation in outline form will ultimately prove more useful than will a long-winded exposition on each element of concern. Certain topics may suffer somewhat from this brevity but readers will possess a concise list of important concepts which they can commit to memory. These, along with the time-tested virtues taught by Mom and Dad, are still the key to long term success.

Certainly there are additional points which other people might include in this list, but if you can practice each of the ones mentioned here as if they were second nature, I have no doubt that you will be successful in business without need of further instruction.

1. Develop an overall business strategy and stick to it until proven wrong.
2. Don't be impatient; building a highly profitable business

usually requires several years.

3. Study problems carefully and then rely upon your own judgement rather than that of others.

4. Be realistic; have a factual basis for your decisions. Analyze data in numerical form whenever possible.

5. Be enthusiastic, even under trying circumstances you should be able to maintain a positive outlook if you are truly interested in what you are doing.

6. Don't procrastinate. Tackle unpleasant jobs at their proper time and get them out of the way.

7. Ask questions and learn. Don't be afraid to show your ignorance.

8. Learn to think and communicate precisely. Don't leave things up in the air.

9. Knowledge is power. Stay abreast of new developments. Read and study all about your business. It is a false economy to be miserly with your educational program.

10. Plan ahead and anticipate upcoming developments rather than reacting to them after the fact.

11. Make your business compatible with a satisfying personal life.

12. Allow adequate time to think and develop management strategies for your business.

13. Long term success is built upon repeat business. Treat customers fairly to promote enduring relationships.

14. Manage risk. Always make decisions with an appreciation of the risks involved.

15. Rely upon proven products, techniques, and policies for everyday business operation. Innovations should be introduced on a trial basis first.

16. Efficient repetition of processes, actions, and policies without the need for constant supervision is key to profitable

business operation. Avoid "one of a kind" situations which are the rightful domain of the artist.

17. Structure your business so that every aspect is as predictable as possible. Intelligent decisions cannot be made without a predictable atmosphere.

18. Do not overextend yourself financially. When decisions are made in a state of financial panic, they are wrong more often than right.

19. Don't allow the actions of competitors to unduly influence your business decisions.

20. Increase your personal efficiency by managing other people effectively and by using labor saving technology where it is economically applicable.

21. Control the destiny of your business by being as self-sufficient as is reasonably possible. Initial cost is not always the primary consideration. Predictability and quality control are often most easily accomplished through internal control.

22. Concentrate upon business niches which most effectively utilize your expertise, inclination, and resources.

23. Integrate the individual aspects of your business so that the whole functions as efficiently as possible. If a particular aspect doesn't not lend itself to integration, think about eliminating it.

24. Focus upon accumulating successful business programs over the long term. Even if you add only one small profit center each year, it won't take long before there is a substantial income flow.

25. Always be aware of the value of your time.

26. Be frugal; never pay more than necessary.

Personal Note from the Author:

Over the years, I have seen many competitors come and go. My personal appraisal of why such a number have failed is that they were too short-sighted and too impetuous to aim for solid, year-after-year growth. They were characterized by a "boom and bust" mentality:

Too much borrowing to finance questionable programs, too much expansion without a proven market, too much machinery they couldn't afford, too much high priced advertising, and not enough analysis of key business decisions.

Survival in business is quite similar to survival in the world of nature: animals and plants normally evolve slowly and step-by-step because large new characteristics are usually out of step with the established environment.

Chapter 12

HOW TO FINANCE A NEW BUSINESS

There are many reasons why only a small fraction of all the business ventures dreamed up by people ever get off the ground. One of the major difficulties lies in getting the money together for a start. Fortunately, many horticulturally-based businesses require only a minimal grubstake. The amount of money you will need to start with depends upon the type of business, how large you wish to begin, how much expense you can avoid by substituting hard work, and the amount of usable resources you already possess.

No matter how you finance a new business, don't start out too big. Limit your risk by beginning small and then grow as you gain experience. Whether you borrow money or finance the venture yourself, plan realistically so that you have enough capital to see the project through to completion.

A good deal of early expenses can be avoided if you work a little harder and improvise by salvaging and recycling useful materials. However, carrying this form of economy too far can exhaust your energy and slow down the project more than the savings are worth.

I do not expect that the following discussion of financial sources is complete, but it does touch upon the most promising avenues. Whatever financial source you wish to employ, the lender will be more favorably disposed if a well-conceived business and financial plan is offered in support of your application. Most commercial or government lenders have trained staff and written materials to help you prepare such a proposal. Organizing your thoughts into a coherent plan is not only essential from the lender's point of view, but it is a great aid in clarifying your own vision of the future.

If you read the newspapers or listen to news programs, the inevitability of cost overruns will come as no surprise. Sloppy preparation of cost estimates is one reason for this phenomenon, but the major culprit is the impossibility of anticipating every small expense which may be encountered in a project. Your financial projections should include a fund for unexpected expenses, especially during the first years of business when money is tight and your experience is limited. I normally anticipate a 5-10% cost overrun for specific projects, even though I have been in business for over 30 years. This is in addition to a small miscellaneous fund which I set aside for every cost estimate.

Most people who plan to start a horticultural business probably already have a job or other sources of income. I strongly suggest that you plan new business activities to coexist for a time with your present employment. The extra outside income will take part of the financial strain off you and may provide important health care benefits.

Of course, there will be a point where it is impossible to continue burning the candle at both ends. A decision must be made to abandon one or the other. For some people, this is a very traumatic event; making a choice between the security of a good job and the dream of owning a successful business is not an easy task. Hopefully, your business will be so profitable that no great sacrifice in security need be made.

Another means of minimizing the money you will need to get started is to postpone some major expenses as long as possible. This may be accomplished by renting or leasing as much as is practical or by just plain doing without until absolutely necessary. Not only does this save initial capital, but it lets you gain important experience before committing to major purchases. The following avenues represent the most frequently employed means of obtaining small business capital.

Relatives and friends

Aside from personal assets, this is the most common source of start up funds for small business people. It shouldn't be! You may jeopardize close relationships by using friends and relatives as money lenders. Even when the business is a resounding success, and everyone is paid back according to schedule, some strain may be introduced into the relationship. I don't have to tell you what happens if you can't retire the debt as promised.

If you must borrow from family or friends, insist that everything be formally written down just as if you were getting the money from a bank. This will help make sure there are no misconceptions which will come back to haunt you in the future.

Banks and commercial lenders

A person might think the local bank or savings and loan would be a prime source for small business start up funds. Don't get your hopes up! Unless you have iron clad collateral, some type of government loan guarantee, or you catch them at a weak moment, banks are not likely to take a risk on you. Bankers are very conservative and like to make their money on sure bets. Occasionally some form of lending hysteria (one of which took place in the 1980's and precipitated the great savings and loan scandal) overcomes their caution. But then the easy money usually goes to slick talkers or old school chums, rather than well-intentioned people like you and me.

Banks not only desire collateral, they want you to show a demonstrated ability to repay the loan. Taking possession of your belongings is a messy business (and it may be expensive), and it isn't what they really like to do. They would much rather receive their payments on schedule. So even if you have adequate collateral but cannot show a steady income source adequate to meet monthly loan payments, don't count on getting a loan.

There are of course various other private companies who are in the business of lending money. Some of these are more-or-less on par with banks or credit unions as far as their integrity and amount of interest charged, and most are reliable firms but charge higher rates than banks, while a few private lenders border upon being unscrupulous, at least with regard to the interest charged.

While banks and commercial lenders are not especially receptive to start up business loans, they are extraordinarily receptive to home improvement loans. It may well be that you can obtain financing for certain business-related expenses through a home loan. Most banks are glad to extend credit for recreational greenhouses if the structure meets certain criteria. Improvements for nursery and perennial beds might also be eligible. Loans for small garden type equipment are available not only through the bank, but most all large stores dealing in this type of merchandise have a time payment program which is easy to utilize.

Home improvement and similar type loans are relatively easy to arrange and can take a good deal of the hassle out of getting the money approved for a project. But I must make it clear that providing false information for loan purposes is against the law.

As long as the improvements are made according to specifications in the loan agreement, you will have no problems. But applying for home improvement money, and then using it for totally unrelated purposes, exposes you to legal action by the lender. The improvement must be for a bonafide purpose which the lending agency gives approval. Incidental use later in your home business will not upset them.

There are several types of assets upon which banks or other types of commercial lenders will loan money. Your home, vehicles, major equipment, land, life insurance cash value, stocks, and bonds may be suitable as collateral. This depends upon the policies of the loaning institution.

Guaranteed loans

Because commercial banks and lending institutions are reluctant to supply small business start up money, various government agencies often act as guarantors of these type of loans. You still borrow the money from a local source, but all or part of the loan repayment is guaranteed by government agencies. The Small Business Administration is perhaps the best known of these agencies but there are several other federal programs and numerous individual state and local government counterparts. (State Farm Loan Boards, Community Development Authorities, Federal Loans for Rural Development, etc.)

If you are located in a basically agricultural area, the local county agent can give you a line on various agricultural loan programs offered by state and federal agencies. And in cities there are all types of programs for minorities, disadvantaged persons, and neighborhood improvement. No matter who you are, chances are good that some special program exists to help you get started in business. It is up to you to do the footwork, and locate the specific program which suits your needs best. Seldom does anyone walk up and give you the money, you have to find out where it is and then ask for it.

Since the local bank is often the conduit through which these governmental loans are channeled, the loan department is a good place to visit for preliminary information.

Most of these sponsored loans cost less interest than a similar commercial loan, but they may involve more paperwork since the government is involved.

In the past few years, many communities and counties have become heavily involved in economic development. Some of them actually make funds available for new and existing businesses, while some may only offer tax breaks, technical information, or low-cost locations. State governments also offer similar programs. If you live in a small town or small state, these programs can sometimes be more easily arranged since you (or your close acquaintances) may actually know people who have a contact with the programs. Personal relations are often important in getting a good break.

Financial grants

Grants are the best financial aid you can receive. As the name implies, you are not required to pay the money back. It is free if you qualify. Needless to say, there is less likelihood of finding a grant than of obtaining a loan.

Many governmental agencies have small business grants available. These grants mainly cultivate opportunity for disadvantaged population groups and individuals. Some grants are awarded with the idea of stimulating new technologies or to support particular industries. At the present time, the ecological movement provides the impetus for a favorable outlook concerning grant availability for horticultural projects.

If you live in an economically depressed area, there may be a good deal of economic development aid available through state and local agencies. These entities are perhaps the best source of grants for the ordinary person who has no special disabilities or needs. Loans through these avenues are even easier to obtain and usually carry a low interest rate. Economic development grants may be used to finance any stage of a business, but they are commonly awarded to help businesses plan the feasibility and marketing of products, or to train and hire local workers for the new enterprise.

As with loans, it is up to you to find out what grants might be available in your area. If you are associated with or know of a particular special interest group, this is a good place to begin inquiring. Your city and state government may have personnel who specialize in helping citizens locate grant sources. The local county agent's office will be able to point you towards possible grant money in the areas of horticulture, agriculture, home economics, education, etc.

Local educational institutions such as community colleges may be able to steer you in the right direction. Most colleges have a grants coordinator, and, while they may specialize in educational matters, it is highly likely they have information pertaining to your needs or can put you in contact with the proper people.

Public libraries usually have a data base which can be accessed to locate available grants. Ask the librarian if you are not familiar with how to use the facilities.

Since a grant provides something of value for free, you can imagine that the competition is often severe and that the people who seek grants are sometimes looking only for a handout. When you apply for a grant, don't act as if you expect a free lunch — show that you are willing to put something into the project. Often times you will be expected to contribute money to match the grant available — if your venture is viable, this should not be objectionable.

Some grants are not worth the effort — particularly ones which require an extensive application process or which place too many restrictions upon your business activity. Be sure to evaluate these conditions, and be certain of your financial obligations to the granting agency.

Some grants are called grants but contain contractual obligations which require eventual repayment — in effect being more of a deferred loan.

Partners

People become associated together in business for many reasons, but one of the most common factors bringing business partners together is the need for money. Partners may pool their monetary resources or one may contribute most of the money while the other contributes mainly expertise and time.

Partners in business can be a good source of financial help, but they want something which an ordinary lender does not demand: a part of the business. You should think long and hard before mortgaging the future control of your enterprise. If the primary need is for money, rather than some other valuable asset a partner can bring into the business, I would suggest that you exhaust all other means of financing before becoming involved in co-ownership.

Life insurance, stocks, bonds, retirement accounts

Like many people, you may have assets which can be borrowed against almost automatically — if the assets are in the proper form and in easily accessible accounts.

Many stock and bond brokers will allow you to "margin" (borrow) against your stocks and bonds. This process is usually ridiculously easy. They may also allow you to do the same thing with retirement securities or CDs. In most cases, you can simply sign a "Margin Agreement" (which your brokerage house sends out) and then have the representative place your assets in a special "Margin Account." It really is that easy if you qualify for such accounts. Your broker can easily tell you the details in 5 minutes over the phone. All brokerage houses differ in their policies somewhat — check out several. You can easily switch your securities from one to another house by simply signing a transfer form.

The argument may be made that if you have extensive stock, bond, and retirement assets — you do not need to borrow money. This may be true to some small extent, but there are many situations in which it is wise to borrow money for good projects rather than doing without, or it may be better to borrow short term rather than selling other assets to provide capital. I have several margin accounts which I can utilize by simply making out a check drawn against the account.

Of course, margin accounts must be used only for good purposes, otherwise you can find yourself in hot water quickly. It is just like overdrawing a checking account. And you should not choose a broker simply because they provide easy access to margin money. A broker should be selected mainly because they offer the best services related to investment vehicles. You must understand that when borrowing against securities, the money is coming out of your portfolio—which will be worth less until you replace the borrowed amount. And the broker is charging interest on every dollar he loans you.

Margin accounts should be utilized only by persons who are sophisticated enough financially to use them safely. It takes discipline to properly loan yourself money by making out margin checks.

Retirement accounts and life insurance equity are assets which can be easily used as loan collateral. Your banker or stockbroker can tell you quickly how to borrow against retirement accounts. Life insurance loans can be made through the bank or directly with the insurance representative. The cash value or loan value of insurance policies at various prescribed dates is usually found in tables which accompany your policy.

Credit from suppliers

In my estimation, supplier credit is the most useful, most economical, and easiest way to obtain financing for your business. Suppliers are eager to sell you products and they normally have a ready made line of credit if you have a good personal credit history and comply with minimal credit application procedures. Many suppliers will rely upon their personal evaluation of you if you visit them beforehand.

Remember, every supplier has competitors to worry about. If one company won't extend credit, ask another until you find someone who is more eager to do business. Credit policies vary greatly from one supplier to another. Some will give you the fifth degree, while others will allow you to charge with little more than a short personal visit.

The best way to obtain supplier credit is to prepare a credit history and obtain references from your bankers and other credible people who know you. Then arrange a personal interview with the supplier — this face to face encounter is important. It is easy to say "no" over the phone, but, unless there are compelling reasons, the answer will be "yes" in person.

If you are going into business, start developing supplier credit 6 months ahead. Visiting with the company's salesman is a good start; he or she is always anxious to find a new customer. Talk over your plans with salespersons and ask their advice. You will often learn new things about the field, and, even if you don't, the salesperson is the first step towards obtaining credit, sometimes it is the only one necessary.

Starting early allows you to make a few small orders on credit and then pay for them on time — this may be slightly inconvenient, but it establishes your credit record with the company before you need to purchase supplies worth thousands of dollars. Chances are that with 3 or 4 previous purchases you can develop an almost unlimited credit line before you really need it.

As you develop a larger number of supplier credit accounts, it is not difficult to see that you could have the equivalent of a $100,000 loan which is interest free. By working your inventory carefully, you may not require money from other sources. Many larger horticultural companies sometimes have a $100,000 credit line with only one particular supplier and similar credit with several others. Even if you have only a small business to start you can see that a $1,000 to $5,000 credit line would not be considered unusual at a supply house.

Most suppliers have a net 30 days credit policy. This means that you have 30 days from the date of shipping until payment must be made. In many cases, this payment period may be extended to 60 or 90 days. In the agricultural and horticultural industry, it is not unusual for terms to be extended to cover the entire growing and marketing season — this may be 6 months or longer. Be sure to ask your suppliers about their "time dated terms" or "growing season terms." Not all will have them but a large number do.

Of course, the supplier has his cost of financing your orders priced into the merchandise. You will likely be paying a hidden interest charge, but in most cases this charge is less than what a bank or other source might want for a similar loan — and the supplier is very anxious to set up your credit if you will only supply convincing reasons of your credit worthiness.

This is the beauty of supplier credit: they are almost begging you to use their credit line while banks and other institutions may act as if you are somehow an inferior human being as you approach them for a loan. And suppliers are in your industry — they already believe it is a great business. You don't have to convince them that horticulture is a bonafide member of American industry (this is often a stumbling block at other lending agencies). Banks sometimes refuse to make horticultural loans because they don't regard such ventures as part of the mainstream business community — bankers are very conservative, and they don't like to get involved in anything they haven't seen a hundred times before.

There is another plus to supplier credit — you may often be able to extend the terms easily by simply not paying your bill on time. Although most suppliers specify that they charge interest on unpaid balances, many do not make a policy of actually trying to collect it. If your terms state net 30 days, you can often pay the bill within 60 days and the supplier will still be happy. The downside of not paying on time is that you risk alienating a good source of credit — don't employ this tactic too often, and don't do it without good reason.

There are several points to summarize again before leaving the subject of supplier credit.

- This is your best source of cheap, easy credit without restrictive conditions.
- Set up supplier credit early.
- Suppliers are anxious to do business. You are in the driver's seat if you take the time to convince them of your credit worthiness.
- The supplier believes in horticultural business already, other loan sources probably do not.
- Supplier credit is often free— in most cases you would pay the same price even if you paid cash.
- Know your supplier and salesperson personally; it is hard to deny a friend.
- Be sure to ask about extended terms.
- Suppliers vary greatly in their response to new credit accounts — shop until you find ones that are accommodative.

Leasing

Many people find that leasing vehicles, equipment, and facilities is an effective means of obtaining the things they need to run a business. Of course there are many requirements which cannot be obtained by leasing (consumable items such as inventory, labor costs, utilities, etc.). Although leasing is quite similar to borrowing, there are some important differences. Leasing costs are generally treated differently for tax purposes — the entire cost of leasing often is taken as business expense during the year the expense was incurred. In many cases, the lease may be terminated while the item still has considerable value; therefore, the person leasing is not obligated financially for the entire original cost. Standard leasing programs are available for many types of equipment (most notably for vehicles and similar mobile machines). These programs are often more convenient than applying for a conventional loan.

In recent years a few leasing companies have offered programs specifically set up for horticultural businesses. To my knowledge, these programs are intended for larger operators and will not be of much use for beginners who need only a few thousand dollars worth of equipment.

Unless you operate under particular circumstances where leasing may be advantageous, you are generally better off to borrow money at good rates and purchase the equipment outright. Only an analysis of each situation can show whether leasing or borrowing is a better deal.

Renting facilities and equipment differs from leasing mainly in the time span which the items are utilized.

It is seldom an advantage to rent for long periods. Renting is helpful in some cases where you want to make certain a particular item will work well in your operation before it is actually purchased

Venture capital and stock offerings

I mention these means of obtaining capital mainly to tell you to forget about them unless you plan an extremely large horticultural operation. Transactions of $1,000,000 are small potatoes for venture capital and stock offerings. Much larger deals are more often the rule.

Deferred labor costs

Under certain conditions, you may wish to consider obtaining labor for your operation by offering specific workers a future share in the business in place of a current weekly wage. This amounts to taking on partners and should be approached with a good deal of caution. It is not a good idea unless there are overwhelming benefits.

Credit cards

Everyone can make use of credit cards to some extent when running a business. Most of you are probably more familiar with this type of financial instrument than I am, so I will not comment at length other than to say money borrowed by using credit cards is usually much more expensive than arranging a commercial loan.

The big advantage to credit cards is the convenient and near universal availability of them. And, at present, some pretty hefty credit lines can be arranged by this means. Of course, the ease with which credit cards are obtained and used is always a danger for inexperienced or poorly disciplined people. Personally, I use credit cards only for daily incidental expenses or for travel — and I have arranged for a good line of credit through them for emergency purposes only.

Free money advertised

No doubt most of you have seen many headlines in various magazines proclaiming the availability of **Free Money** or **Free Grants** or **Immediate Loans**. While I cannot judge all these offers, I can say that the few I have checked into are no more than scams directed at people who have nothing better to do than chase rainbows. If you are serious about running a real business, forget about these free money programs and direct your efforts to more realistic work.

GET STARTED NOW

I must emphasize in conclusion that getting an early start at arranging financing for your business can make the difference between success and failure. Not only does an early start assure that the money is available when you need it but also at the lowest possible expense.

In many cases, there is no better way to become familiar with business financing than to plunge in and make a trial run with various avenues you might wish to employ. This method of learning the ropes costs only some of your time. There is no obligation on your part unless you sign legal papers (hopefully you will not do that until you are thoroughly familiar with each alternative).

Personal Note from the Author:

Most businesses operate on credit to a large extent. I can't argue with the benefits of this policy – it allows for faster growth and may help a business get off the ground which would otherwise never be started.

However, excess borrowing is the death knell for many entrepreneurs. If you are heavily in debt, the first crisis may put you under. And believe me, even a healthy business will eventually face trying times.

Be safe: avoid borrowing more than is absolutely essential and be sure you have a realistic long term plan for repayment.

Chapter 13

COPING WITH SUCCESS

Some persons strive to succeed for years and then find themselves at loose ends when the objective is finally achieved. One way to avoid this "wrecked by success" syndrome is to begin envisioning future goals even during the early stages of your present venture.

Start asking questions about how large you want the business to become, how much time you want to devote to it once it is established, and how it will be disposed of in the future. If you consider these and other important points long before they develop into actualities, you may find that the answers become evident as you make progress toward more immediate goals.

Success in business is not easy to achieve, and it is a shame to see so many good people squander the work of a lifetime simply because they failed to plan for the demands which prosperity places upon them. Good fortune doesn't last forever, so I suggest that you ensure the success you have achieved by paying all debts and establishing an emergency fund for the inevitable bouts of bad luck which everyone is bound to encounter. Then new personal and commercial projects can be pursued if you feel the need for further accomplishment.

Perhaps the most intractable problem successful business persons encounter is the need to delegate responsibility. The very characteristics which enable small business people to succeed in the first place often prevent them from allowing other individuals to begin shouldering some of the load. No business can continue to grow unless authority and responsibility are passed on to subordinates.

Even if you do not care to have a business which keeps on growing indefinitely, it will be necessary to delegate responsibility so that you have time to enjoy present accomplishments. Begin early by developing the habit of letting someone else take care of routine daily activities. If you don't, the increasing demands of business will become suffocating.

Developing a business organization rather than continuing to operate as a "one man show" will not only enable you to have time for personal enjoyments, it will ensure that the business you build is a marketable entity which an owner can operate without becoming entangled in daily technical details. A profitable small business is worth a good deal of money, and it can be made even more valuable by developing a management and labor team which can run the business with a minimum of direction. A business should be thought of not only as a source of immediate income, but as a financial asset which may someday be sold.

I hope this book has provided you with a clear outline of how to get started and be successful in a horticultural specialty business. There is surely an Earth-friendly enterprise which will prove both profitable and enjoyable if you wish to try your luck.

Remember, business should add to the enjoyment of life rather than greedily consuming all your energies and free time. Make sure you never lose sight of this important concept. If you love plants, making money in a horticulturally-related business can fulfill monetary needs without compromising aesthetic and spiritual values which should provide the basis for a good life.

Appendix

USEFUL INFORMATION

Media ph for soilless organic media	
Extremely low	4.5 or less
Slightly low	5.0 to 5.1
Optimum	5.2 to 5.5
Slightly high	5.6 to 5.8
Extremely high	6.9+

Water quality rating			
Water quality rating	Relative salt content	Reading in micromhos	Reading in ppm
Excellent	low	0-250	167
Good to fair	medium	250-750	167-500
Fair to poor	medium-high	750-2250	500-
Poor	excessive	2250+	1500+

Appendix

Liquid measure		
1 level tablespoon	=	3 level teaspoons
1 cupful	=	.5 pint 8 fluid ounces 16 tablespoons
1 fluid ounce (U.S.)	=	2 tablespoons 29.57 mililiters
1 pint (U.S.)	=	16 fluid ounces 2 cupfuls 473.2 mililiters
1 quart (U.S.)	=	32 fluid ounces 2 pints .9463 liter
1 gallon (U.S.)	=	128 fluid ounces 8 pints 4 quarts .1337 cubic feet 231 cubic inches 3.785 liters

Dry measure

3 level teaspoons	=	1 level tablespoon
16 level tablespoons	=	1 cupful
2 cupfuls	=	1 pint
1 dry pint	=	33.6003 cu. in.
1 dry pint	=	.01994 cu. ft.
1 dry pint	=	.55061 liter
2 pints	=	1 quart
1 dry quart	=	67.2006 cu. in.
8 quarts	=	1 peck
4 pecks	=	1 bushel

Ounces to Grams conversion

Ounces	Grams	Ounces	Grams
1/2	14.175	1/256	.111
1	28.349	1/128	.221
2	56.698	1/64	.443
		1/32	.886
Seed quantities often		1/16	1.772
measured in these sizes >>		1/8	3.544
		1/4	7.087

Decimal gallon/ounce equivalents	
.25 gallon =	32 ounces 1 quart
.5 gallon =	64 ounces 2 quarts
.75 gallon =	96 ounces 3 quarts
1.0 gallon =	128 ounces 4 quarts

Percent to ratio conversions		
2.0%	=	1:50
1.0%	=	1:100
0.8%	=	1:128
0.5%	=	1:200
∧	∧	∧

Frequently used fertilizer injection ratios.

Loan repayment table
Term Amount: $10,000 Interest: 7%
5 years: $198.02/per month 10 years: $116.11 15 years: $89.89 20 years: $77.53 25 years: $70.68

Pot volumes	
Pot size	Number filled by 1 cubic yard
4" standard	1,293
4" azalea	1,616
6" standard	397
6" azalea	488.7
8" st.	176

Farenheit/Celsius conversion

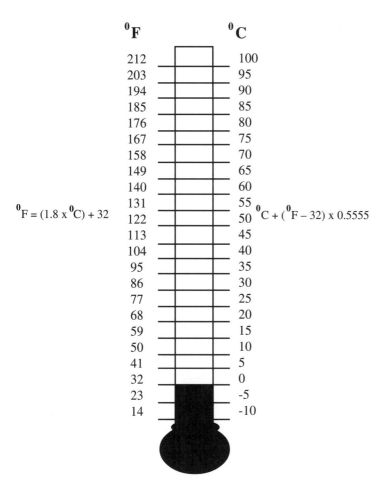

^{0}F

^{0}C

^{0}F = (1.8 x ^{0}C) + 32

^{0}C + (^{0}F − 32) x 0.5555

^{0}F	^{0}C
212	100
203	95
194	90
185	85
176	80
167	75
158	70
149	65
140	60
131	55
122	50
113	45
104	40
95	35
86	30
77	25
68	20
59	15
50	10
41	5
32	0
23	-5
14	-10

Metric equivalent		
1 square centimeter	=	.1550 square inches
1 square inch	=	6.452 square centimeters
1 square decimeter	=	.1076 square foot
1 square foot	=	9.2903 sq. decimeters
1 square meter	=	1.196 square yards
1 square yard	=	.8361 square meter
1 acre	=	160 square rods
1 square rod	=	.00625 acre

Approx. Metric equivalents		
1 decimeter	=	4 inches
1 meter	=	1.1 yards
1 kilometer	=	5/8 mile
1 kilogram	=	2 1/5 pounds
1 metric ton	=	2,204.6 pounds

Metric vs. English measurement

1 centimeter	=	.3937 inch
1 inch	=	2.54 centimeters
1 foot	=	30.48 centimeters
1 meter	=	39.37 inches
1 meter	=	100 centimeters
1 meter	=	1.094 yards
1 meter	=	1,000 millimeters
1 yard	=	.914 meter
1 mile	=	1609.344 meters
1 kilometer	=	1000 meters
1 kilometer	=	.62317 miles
1 sq. centimeter	=	.155 sq. inches
1 cubic centimeter	=	.061 cubic inches
1 fluid ounce	=	30 milliliters
1 liter	=	1.057 quarts

LD$_{50}$ – Probable lethal quanities of orally ingested substances related to various human LD 50 ranges

LD 50 : The lethal dosage for 50% of test animals expressed as milligrams of toxicant per kilogram of body weight.

EPA category rating	EPA pesticide label "signal" word
I. Highly Hazardous	**Danger–Poison**
II. Moderately Hazardous	**Warning**
III. Slightly Hazardous	**Caution**
IV. Relatively Nonhazardous	**Caution**

LD 50 range	Quantity of substance ingested orally
I. 0 to 50 mg.	**A taste or a few drops.**
II. 50 to 500 mg.	**1 teaspoon to 2 tablespoons or 1 ounce.**
III. 500 to 5000 mg.	**2 tablespoons or 1 ounce to 1 pint or pound.**
IV. 5000 mg or over.	**Over 1 pint or pound.**

Lethal Doses of common substances
Aspirin   1750 mg
Caffeine   200
Nicotine   50
Tylenol   3700

Area determinations

Triangle

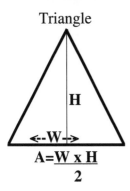

$$A=\frac{W \times H}{2}$$

Rectangle

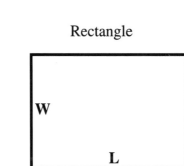

$$A=W \times L$$

Circle

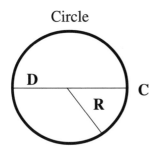

A=3.142 x R xR
C=3.142 x D
R=D÷2
D=2 x R
(Pi=3.142)

Trapezoid

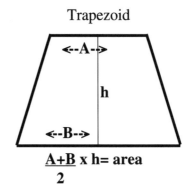

$$\frac{A+B}{2} \times h= area$$

U.S. Cooperative Extension Service

Write to the main office in your state for helpful literature, information on soil testing, or specific information concerning your particular crop.

Alabama
Auburn University
Auburn, AL 36849

Alaska
University of Alaska
Fairbanks, AK 99701

Arizona
University of Arizona
Tucson, AZ 85721

Arkansas
P.O. Box 391
Little Rock, AR 72203

California
University of California
2200 University Ave.
Berkeley, CA 94720

Colorado
Colorado State University
Fort Collins, CO 80523

Connecticut
University of Connecticut
Storrs, CT 06269

Delaware
University of Delaware
Newark, DE 19716

District of Columbia
Federal City College
1424 K. Street NW
Washington, D.C. 20005

Florida
University of Florida
Gainesville, FL 32611

U.S. Cooperative Extension Service (cont.)

Georgia
University of Georgia
Athens, GA 30602

Hawaii
University of Hawaii
Honolulu, HI 96822

Idaho
University of Idaho
Morill Hall
Moscow, ID 83843

Illinois
University of Illinois
Urbana, IL 61801

Iowa
Iowa State University
Ames, IA 50011

Kansas
Kansas State University
Manhattan, KS 66506

Kentucky
University of Kentucky
Lexington, KY 40546

Louisiana
Louisiana State University
Baton Rouge, LA 70803

Maine
University of Maine
Orono, ME 04469

Maryland
University of Maryland
College Park, MD 20742

Massachusetts
University of Mass.
Amherst, MA 48824

Michigan
Michigan State University
East Lansing, MI 48824

Minnesota
University of Minnesota
St. Paul, MN 55455

Mississippi
Mississippi State Univ.
Mississippi State, MS
39762

U.S. Cooperative Extension Service (cont.)

Missouri
University of Missouri
Columbia, MO 65211

Montana
Montana State University
Bozeman, MT 59717

Nebraska
University of Nebraska
Lincoln, NE 68588

Nevada
University of Nevada
Reno, NV 89557

New Hampshire
Univ. of New Hampshire
Taylor Hall
Durham, NH 03824

New Jersey
Rutgers — The State Univ.
New Brunswick, NJ 08903

New Mexico
New Mexico State Univ.
Las Cruces, NM 88003

New York
New York State Col. of Ag.
Ithaca, NY 14853

North Carolina
North Carolina State Univ.
Raleigh, NC 27695

North Dakota
North Dakota State Univ.
Fargo, ND 58105

Ohio
Ohio State University
Columbus, OH 43210

Oklahoma
Oklahoma State Univ.
Stillwater, OK 74078

Oregon
Oregon State University
Corvallis, OR 97331

Pennsylvania
Pennsylvania State Univ.
University Park, PA 16802

U.S. Cooperative Extension Service (cont.)

Puerto Rico
University of Puerto Rico
Rio Piedras, Puerto Rico
00931

Rhode Island
University of Rhode Island
Kingston, RI 02881

South Carolina
Clemson University
Clemson, SC 29634

South Dakota
South Dakota State Univ.
Brookings, SD 57007

Tennessee
University of Tennessee
P.O. Box 1071
Knoxville, TN 37996

Texas
Texas A&M University
College Station, TX 77843

Utah
Utah State University
Logan, UT 84322

Vermont
University of Vermont
Burlington, VT 05405

Virginia
Virginia Polytechnic
Institute and State Univ.
Blacksburg, VA 24601

Washington
Washington State Univ.
Pullman, WA 99164

West Virginia
West Virginia University
Morgantown, WV 26506

Wisconsin
University of Wisconsin
Madison, WI 53706

Wyoming
University of Wyoming
Box 3354, Univ. Station
Laramie, WY 82071

Internet addresses

**United States
Department of Agriculture
Cooperative State Research and Extension Service**
http://www.reeusda.gov/new/csrees.htm

**United States
Department of Agriculture**
http://www.usda.gov

**United States
Agriculture Statistics**
http://www.usda.gov/nass/

**United States
Department of Agriculture
Plants Database**
http://www.plants.usda.gov/plants/plntmenu.html

Small Business Administration
http://www.sbaonline.sba.gov

**United States
Department of Commerce**
http://www.doc.gov

National Weather Service
http://www.nws.noaa.gov

Internet addresses (cont.)

Plant Web
http://www.plantweb.com
(an excellent source for
horticultural links)

American Horticultural Society
http://www.ahs.org/

American Society of Horticultural Science
http://www.ashs.org/

**American Nursery and Landscape
Association**
http://www.anla.org

Associated Landscape Contractors of America
http://www.alca.org

Southern Nursery Association
http://www.sna.org

National Gardening Association
http://www.garden.org/nga/

LITERATURE

American Nurseryman
American Nurseryman Pub. Co.
77 West Washington St. #2100
Chicago, IL 60602
(312)782-5505
1-800-621-5727

American Vegetable Grower
Meister Publishing Co.
37733 Euclid Ave.
Willoughby, OH 44094
(216) 942-2000
1-800-572-7740

Floral Mass Marketing
205 W. Wacker Drive Ste. 1040
Chicago, IL 60606
(312) 739-5000

Florist's Review
(312) 782-5505
1-800-621-5727

Flowers
11444 Olympic Blvd.
4th Floor
Los Angeles, CA 90064
(310) 231-9199

Flower News
205 W. Wacker Drive Ste. 1040
Chicago, IL 60606
(312) 739-5000

Garden Supply Retailer
One Chilton Way
Radnor, PA 19089
(610) 964-4269

Greenhouse Business
1951 Rohlwing Rd. Suite B
Rolling Meadows, IL 60008
(847) 870-1576

Greenhouse Grower
Meister Publishing Co.
37733 Euclid Ave.
Willoughby, OH 44094
(216) 942-2000
1-800-572-7740

Greenhouse Product News
Scranton Gillette Comm., Inc.
380 E. Northwest Hwy. Ste. 200
Des Plaines, IL 60016
(847) 298-6622

Grower Talks
P.O. Box 9
Batavia, IL 60510
(888) 201-1962

Growers Press, Inc.
P.O. Box 189
Princeton, B.C. Canada
VOX 1WO
1(250) 295-7755

Herbs for Health, Also Herb Companion. And other Herb books
Interweave Press
201 E. 4th St.
Loveland, CO 80537
(970) 669-7672
1-800-645-3675

Interior Landscape
American Nurseryman Publ. Co.
77 W. Washington St., Ste. 2100
Chicago, IL 60602
(312) 782-5505
1-800-621-5727

Nursery Retailer
Brantwood Publications
2410 Northside Drive
Clearwater, FL 33761
(727) 796-3877

The Growing Edge
P.O. Box 1027
Corvallis, OR 97339
(541) 757-2511

The Herb Quarterly
P.O. Box 689
San Anselmo, CA 94979
1-800-371-HERB

The Soilless Grower
Hydroponic Society of America
P.O. Box 1183
El Cerito, CA 94530
(510) 232-2323

All the following are publications of :

Branch-Smith Publishing
120 St. Louis Avenue
Fort Worth, TX 76104
(817) 332-8236 or 1-800-433-5612

Garden Center Products & Supplies
Garden Center Merchandising & Management
Greenhouse Management & Production
Nursery Management & Production
SAF Magazine

Horticulture- Magazine of American Gardening
98 N. Washington St.
Boston, MA 02114-1913
(617) 742-5600

Fine Gardening
63 S. Main St.
P.O. Box 5506
Newtown, CT 06470-5506
(203) 426-8171

The American Gardener
American Horticultural Society
7931 E. Boulevard Drive
Alexandria, VA 22308-1300
(703) 768-5700

National Gardening
Magazine of The National Gardening Assoc.
180 Flynn Ave.
Burlington, VT 05401
1-800-538-7476

Entrepreneur Magazine
2392 Morse Ave.
Irvine, CA 92614
(949) 261-2325

**Home Business
Magazine**
9582 Hamilton Ave.
Suite 368
Huntington Beach, CA 92646
(714) 968-0331

**American Horticultural
Therapy Association**
9220 Wightman Rd.
Suite 3000
Gaithersburg, MD 20879
(303) 331-3862

People Plant Connection
(303) 820-3151

Journal of Theraputic Horticulture
(303) 820-3151

INDEX

BOOKS BY ANDMAR PRESS

Andmar Press offers the following books by Dr. Jozwik about opportunities and methods in commercial horticulture. Mail order delivery to your door is available. Each purchase is fully guaranteed. Cash refunds are honored for any reason if the original invoice is presented.

The Greenhouse and Nursery Handbook
A Complete Guide to Growing and Selling Ornamental Container Plants.

Everything you need to know about how to grow and sell ornamental plants is clearly presented in this large, illustrated volume. The culture of hundreds of bedding plants, flowering pot plants, foliage plants, trees, shrubs, and perennials is covered from A to Z. Basic environmental factors like fertilizers, moisture, temperature, insects and diseases, and soil are explained in terms everyone can understand. *The Greenhouse and Nursery Handbook* is an absolute must for every horticulturist whether their interests are commercial or recreational. Hardback $97 plus $7.00 shipping. 806 pages.

Perennial Plants for Profit or Pleasure
How to Grow Perennial Flowers and Herbs for Profit or Personal Landscape Use.

This book details the exact methods necessary to set up a low cost business growing perennial plants—literally in your own backyard. Or you can use the system to provide economical perennials for parks, businesses, garden clubs, churches, or home gardens. Every step of production and marketing is clearly pointed out. Convenient sources for supplies are included for free. $39.95 plus $5.00 shipping. Hardcover. 300 pages.

How to Make Money Growing Plants, Trees, and Flowers.
A Guide to Profitable Earth-Friendly Ventures.
    Outlines the many business opportunities available in horticulture and offers the reader important preliminary information about how to choose a field of interest and how to get started correctly. This book is essential for anyone who needs a concise summary of practical start up advice. $39.95 plus $5.00 shipping. Hardcover. 308 pages.

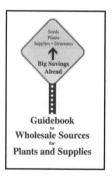

Guidebook to Wholesale Sources for Plants and Supplies
    Tells you how to easily obtain beautiful catalogs from leading wholesale horticultural firms. Complete addresses and telephone numbers included to save you time. The companies listed offer a large selection of wholesale supplies and plants which are available only to established professional growers or persons who wish to begin a horticultural business soon. $9.95 plus $3.00 shipping.

Plants for Profit—*Income Opportunities in Horticulture*

A multifaceted book which presents general information about how to start a horticultural business and then examines details of some specific business and employment opportunities. On site field trip forms are included to familiarize you with the industry. Numerous trade publications are cited for further information. $39.95 plus $5.00 shipping. Hardcover. 304 pages.

The Illustrated Handbook of Landscape Plants— *Includes Trees, Shrubs, Annuals and Perennials.*

An indispensable guide to hundreds of North American ornamental species. Illustrated profusely in color to help both professionals and amateurs plan beautiful and ecologically sound landscapes. Details of size, color, and cultural preferences outlined for each variety. Durable 8½ x 11 hardcover notebook style allows professionals to add their own material and drawings for a full open presentation to customers. $39.95 plus $5.00 shipping.

Visit Our Website@ andmar.com

ORDER BLANK FOR BOOKS

Please send the following books to me. I understand the total order amount below must be transferred to the reverse side of this page where I will indicate my shipping instructions and deduct any allowable postage discount for orders of more than one title.

Quan.	Title	Price	Shipping	Total
_____	*The Greenhouse and* *Nursery Handbook* Hardback Deluxe Edition	$97.00	$7.00	$ _____
_____	*Perennial Plants for* *Profit or Pleasure*	$39.95	$5.00	$ _____
_____	*Make Money Growing Plants,* *Trees, and Flowers*	$39.95	$5.00	$ _____
_____	*Guidebook to Wholesale Sources for* *Plants and Supplies*	$9.95	$3.00	$ _____
_____	*Plants for Profit – Income* *Opportunities in Horticulture*	$39.95	$5.00	$ _____
_____	*The Illustrated Handbook* *of Landscape Plants*	$29.95	$5.00	$ _____

**Total amount due for
titles ordered** .... $ _____

Canadian and foreign orders must be paid by VISA or MasterCard or by money orders denominated in U.S. dollars. Canadian and U.K. orders add $5.00 additional shipping per order. All other foreign orders add $15.00 per order for insured air mail.Orders shipped priority mail where possible.

> **Please transfer the total order amount to the reverse side
> of this page and complete all shipping instructions carefully.
> Enclose full payment by check, credit card, or money order.**

FULL MONEY BACK GUARANTEE

SHIPPING AND PAYMENT FORM

Total book order from reverse side of this page .... $ _____

United States and territories customers subtract a
$2.00 postage discount for each title ordered
after the first book .... $ (_____)

Total amount due in U.S. dollars after postage
discount subtracted .... $ _____

Check type of payment enclosed:
☐ Visa or MC ☐ Money Order

☐ Check (drawn on U.S. Branch)

Andmar Press
West Yellowstone Highway
P.O. Box 217
Mills, WY 82644-0217

Please Print or Type Clearly

Name _____

Company _____

Address _____

_____

City _____

State/Zip _____

Phone (_____) _____
VISA or MC
Full Number _____

Expiration Date _____

FULL MONEY BACK GUARANTEE

**Please review your order on the reverse side of this page to
make sure both the titles and order total are correct.**